THE
PARABLE
OF TEN
PREACHERS

THE PARABLE OF TEN PREACHERS

Thomas H. Troeger

ABINGDON PRESS
Nashville

THE PARABLE OF TEN PREACHERS

This book is printed on recycled, acid-free paper.

Library of Congress Cataloging-in-Publication Data

TROEGER, THOMAS H., 1945-
 The parable of ten preachers / Thomas H. Troeger.
 p. cm.
 Includes bibliographical references and index.
 ISBN 0-687-30030-4 (alk. paper)
 1. Preaching. I. Title
 BV4211.2.T764 1991
 251—dc20   91-28452
                                                  CIP

MANUFACTURED IN THE UNITED STATES OF AMERICA

To the students, pastors, and laypreachers
who have been in my class and seminars
and whose struggles to preach the gospel
have inspired this parable

Contents

Introduction   9

**List of Characters
in Their Order of Appearance**   11

Chapter 1: Remembered Voices
Recalling the Preachers from Our Past   13

Chapter 2: Neglected Voices
Listening to Outsiders   38

Chapter 3: New Voices
Gathering Together All We Have Heard   67

Chapter 4: The Voice Upon the Deep
Hearing Christ in Unexpected Ways   92

Notes   122

Index   127

Introduction

his book is a parable about preaching. I have written it for those who have preached for many years and for those who are just beginning. Most of the action takes place in a homiletics class made up of ten preachers coming from a wide diversity of backgrounds and traditions.

You are invited to become the eleventh member of the class, to consider the sermons you will hear and to imagine yourself entering the energetic class discussions.

Although the narrative and the characters are imaginary, they are based on my work with preachers and seminarians of many different backgrounds and perspectives. The issues that emerge in their sermons and discussions reflect recurring themes in the preaching seminars that I have led throughout the United States and Canada during the last fourteen years.

I am especially indebted to several preachers whom I interviewed at length and who provided me with information and insight to help me create the characters from backgrounds that are different from my own. I have tried to be as true as possible to the spirit of what they told me.

This book was originally the lecture series for "Proclamation '91: Preaching Toward the 21st Century," a national conference sponsored by Cokesbury Seminars at Nashville, Tennessee, April 15–19, 1991. I have incorporated a number of revisions that were suggested to me by pastors who were present for that event to make the book even truer to the actual experience of local congregations.

The characters often quote from various books they are reading. Although my narrative is fiction, the citations are from actual published works. The source of each quotation is given in the notes to each chapter at the end of the book. In addition to this information, the notes sometimes list other books and sources that are not quoted by the characters, but that influenced me as I was developing the book.

I hope that through your imaginative participation in the class you will be helped in your own search to find your most effective voice as a preacher so that you can more effectively proclaim the gospel into the twenty-first century.

Thomas H. Troeger

List of Characters
in Their Order of Appearance

Peter Linden, homiletics professor at the seminary in the city

Katherine Carr, former English professor, now an M.Div. student

Jason Kirk, rural pastor from Clydes Corners

Dorian White Elk, pastor on leave for his D.Min.

Roger Hawkins, suburban pastor from Grafton Heights

Tushika Bronson, city pastor and D.Min. candidate

Marjorie Hudson, former nurse, now an M.Div. student

Isaiah Thompson, former electrical engineer, now a city pastor

Karen Steel, chaplain's assistant and M.Div. student

Edward Hanson, divinity school senior preparing for graduate school

Chung Won Kim, city pastor

You, the reader of this book, with all that you bring to it

Chapter 1

Remembered Voices

Recalling the Preachers from Our Past

Peter Linden put down the book he was reading about new methods of preaching. He gazed at the bold print on the wall calendar above his desk: **January 2000.**
Two, zero, zero, zero.

While Peter's eyes traced the round shape of the giant zeroes, he remembered a spring term exactly ten years ago when he had offered an advanced homiletics seminar entitled "Preachers in Search of Their Voices." The course had looked at the challenges of proclaiming the gospel effectively into the twenty-first century. What kind of "voice" would preachers need in an increasingly pluralistic church and society?

From all of his years of teaching homiletics, Peter was convinced that every preacher has a "voice," a distinctive pattern of substance and expression that can be traced from sermon to sermon. Jeremiah's "voice" is different from Micah's. Luke's "voice" is different from Matthew's. Effective preachers keep searching for their true voices, for the way they can most faithfully express the holy vision that impels their witness to God.[1]

Peter got out of his office chair with the cracked green leather seat and went to the filing cabinet and fished out the course folder, which was already beginning to yellow with age. At the top of the syllabus was part of an editorial that *The Christian Century* had published one hundred years earlier as the 1890s had drawn to a close. Peter had chosen the quotation in order to remind the class what risky business it is to speak for the future:

We believe that the coming century is to witness greater triumphs in Christianity than any previous century has ever witnessed, and that it is to be more truly Christian than any of its predecessors.[2]

Peter's eyes moved from the 1890s quotation back to the new calendar on the wall.

January 2000.

His mind filled with the televised images of a program he had watched during the last the week of 1999. It was a recap of the twentieth century:

Mustard gas drifting over the fields of World War I.
Bodies at Auschwitz.
A mushroom cloud.
Police dogs attacking black demonstrators.
A Vietnamese girl on fire running down the road.
The space shuttle exploding.
Sea gulls covered and choked with oil.
Baghdad on fire.

That century was supposed to have been "more truly Christian than any of its predecessors."

Peter Linden's mind became completely still, like the stillness of a prayer too deep for words.

Then he glanced over the class list for "Preachers in Search of Their Voices." He slowly reread the students' names and listened with his memory for the echo of their speech as they preached and talked in class.

Tashika Bronson
Katherine Carr
Dorian White Elk
Edward Hanson
Roger Hawkins
Marjorie Hudson
Chung Won Kim
Jason Kirk
Karen Steel
Isaiah Thompson

Hearing and seeing each of them in his mind, Peter realized once again that he was no homiletical mechanic who owned a set of universal pulpit wrenches that would fit every preacher's voice and every church's ethos.

Peter found a copy of the opening exercise, which he had passed around the seminar table on the first day of class, back in 1990. There were three questions:

1. What is your best memory of a sermon or preacher that had a positive impact on your life?
2. Why was this sermon or preacher so effective?
3. What do your answers tell you about finding your voice as a preacher for the twenty-first century?

Katherine Carr had been the first to speak. Katherine had taught college English before she felt called to ordained ministry. She had a broad face, pale blue eyes, and wore large dangling earrings that amplified her characteristic gesture of tilting her head to the side when she paused in conversation or during her sermon delivery. She had considered taking a leave of absence because she was pregnant with her first child, and she feared the baby, despite the doctor's predictions, might come before classes were over. She insisted that she always be called Katherine, and not Kathy or Kate.

Katherine began by telling what was going on in her life when she heard the sermon that so powerfully affected her. She had been teaching for three years as a graduate student assistant, finishing up her Ph.D. thesis in between grading freshman essays and teaching the seminars that professors did not want. Although raised in a strong church family—she had been president of the youth fellowship in high school—Katherine had not attended church in years, and for one clear reason: Studies in feminist literary criticism had made her so aware of the patriarchy of Christian Scripture and worship that she could no longer bear to sing the hymns and offer the prayers and listen to the readings with their incessant recital of male names.

Because of her strong church background as a child, Katherine had periodically tried to return to worship, but every time she did, she felt like a daughter raised in a household where the men did all the talking and the women were never listened to.

Katherine remembered vividly the events that led up to her hearing of the sermon that changed her life. The Friday before that Sunday her thesis had been approved, and she had celebrated through the night and into the early hours of Saturday. Then she had gone to bed in the afternoon and slept straight through until Sunday morning. When she climbed out of bed, she was depressed. It was not simply the depression of having overindulged her body on drink and staying up through Friday night. Nor could she fully explain it as the depression of having finally let go of a project that had consumed her energy for the last few years. Both of these contributed to her state of mind, but they did not in themselves provide a sufficient account of what she was feeling.

While she put on the morning coffee, one of her roommates stumbled into the kitchen, inviting Katherine to attend church. Christmas was approaching, and the roommate assured Katherine that the music would be beautiful.

Katherine thought that anything, even going to church, would be better than the emptiness she felt that morning. So she threw on what she thought looked like church, and at 10:00 A.M. found herself entering a sanctuary whose fresh greens and Advent candles reminded her of a childhood on which she thought she had shut and locked the door.

There was, to her surprise, a new hymnal in the racks. It had a cobalt blue cover, and its title in embossed gold was *The United Methodist Hymnal*.

The discovery of this new book after so many years of absence from worship unbalanced Katherine's soul even more than Friday night's celebration. She had thought that coming to church would be an isolated event, a trip down memory lane to a land she had long left behind, stopping here and there for a fond glimpse and closing her eyes on scenes that were too painful.

Her sense of unbalance increased when the preacher who stood in the pulpit to read the gospel and preach the sermon was a woman about her own age, reading from a translation that Katherine had never heard, even though she had been required to take a standard course called "The Bible and Literature."

"In the beginning was the Word," read the preacher from the New Revised Standard Version. "The Word was with God, and the Word was God."

At that moment it began to dawn on Katherine why she was depressed: because she had given all of these years to the study of

16

literature, to the interpretation of words, and to the interpretation of the interpretation of words. Yet always, even at the conclusion of her most brilliant essays that had won the admiration of her peers and professors, she had gone home feeling empty.

Now she began to see why.

In her heart Katherine hoped that human words would flow from something greater than the private vision of an isolated artist, that words would be an expression of the source of language and being: the Word that was at the beginning.

When the woman minister began to preach, she spoke about the Word as being the personification of wisdom, a feminine expression of the divine. For the first time in Katherine's life, she heard a sermon that used feminine pronouns for the Holy One of creation. Tears welled up in her eyes.

It was as though she had returned to her childhood home to find a welcome she had not expected. No longer were the men the only center of attention. Her experience, her belief, her feelings counted as much as theirs.

Near the end of the sermon, the woman preacher had quoted from a book by Sandra Schneiders, *Women and the Word*. The passage moved Katherine so deeply that the next morning she went directly to the university bookstore to find the book. One of her mentors in the English department saw her prowling through the theology section and, trying to be humorous, quipped: "Now that the thesis is over, have you gotten religion?" For a moment Katherine wondered if she were being a fool. She remembered the grumbling she had heard about the sermon as people left the service. She wondered what kind of support she would find in the church for a faith rekindled by feminist theology.

Now on that first day of class, Katherine quoted the passage from Sandra Schneiders's book, words that she had committed to memory with the same fervor that ancient generations had recited the Apostle's Creed:

> We must learn to speak to and about God in the feminine; we must learn to present the religious experience of women as autonomously valid. *The therapy of the religious imagination* is an affair of language in the broad sense of the term, and it is crucial that we

cease to trivialize this issue and begin the long process of conversion from the idolatry of maleness toward the worship of the true God in spirit and in truth.[3]

Katherine told her classmates: "Any preacher's voice worth hearing in the twenty-first century will help to further 'the therapy of the religious imagination.' "

Katherine saw from their faces that some of the students around the table were struggling with what she had said. Their expressions looked like a blend of incomprehension and resistance. So she offered an illustration of what she meant, observing that as she first entered the seminar room she had noticed a brass plaque on the outside of the door, reading:

This room refurbished
through the generous gifts
of the joint council of women's circles
of Asbury Church.

She had opened the door, thinking that perhaps inside there would be a group picture of the women, possibly gathered for some annual meal at their church or maybe a small copy of their charter or a photograph of their founding mothers.

"But instead," Katherine explained as her hand swept toward the walls, "I entered to discover these."

The interior designers who had recently redecorated the seminar room had supplied more than fresh paint, carpet, and chairs. They had reframed a large number of historic black and white photographs, including shots of the seminary's old campus, dominated by a granite Victorian building that was surrounded by high elm trees.

In addition to these larger campus views there were class pictures going back to the late 1890s, still in their original frames. Every senior was surrounded by an oval cutting in a gray matting, so that he was individually set apart, each in his own little cameo. They all looked straight out of the picture with the same serious expression, as if they had put their faces on as carefully as they had tied their black cravats and buttoned the vests on their three-piece Edwardian suits. Underneath every cameo was the student's full name.

Among all the photographs of those preachers who had prepared to preach the gospel into the twentieth century there was no Tashika Bronson or Katherine Carr or Dorian White Elk or Marjorie Hudson or Karen Steel or Chung Won Kim or Isaiah Thompson. They were all young white men.

Even though the room was handsomely painted and appointed, Katherine found it suffocating. To her the room seemed a material manifestation of the patriarchal tradition that had crushed her spirit until she heard that transforming sermon. Katherine said that she hoped preachers would prepare the church for the twenty-first century by "taking everything off the walls and starting again."

Peter scanned the photographs of the early graduates and imagined all of them looking back in horror.

They *were* the past.

No one can change history.

Then Peter heard Katherine continuing. She would not throw out pictures that were already there, but she would see that they were rearranged and vastly augmented by pictures of the women who had made the room possible.

"History," Katherine said, "is choosing what photographs you are going to look at. This room has too limited a selection."

"Well, if it's furnishings that you want to move around, let me tell you about the couch in my church at Clydes Corners," said Jason Kirk. The sound of his voice revealed someone who was skeptical and disturbed by what Katherine had said, but his words indicated that he was not yet ready to deal directly with what unsettled him.

Jason Kirk was sixty-six years old. He gave his age when he introduced himself to the class, observing, "I guess I am the oldest one here." He was a United Methodist pastor who had served nine different charges, most of them in the country or in rural towns. His horn-rimmed glasses matched his neatly trimmed sideburns. He always wore a dark suit to class because he usually combined his hospital calls in the city with his trip to the seminary. There was a sadness in his eyes, as if they had seen so much suffering that the brightest scene would not rekindle their shine. And yet when Jason preached, especially about the healing acts of Jesus, there was a buoyancy in his voice that revealed hope still lived in his heart.

Peter Linden reminded Jason that the goal of the class discussion was to name a sermon or preacher whose impact was positive and to analyze its implications for finding his voice as a preacher.

"I have that right here on the paper," said Jason, tapping the exercise sheet on the table with his index finger. "But if you will let me tell you about the red horsehair couch in our chancel, and the battle over whether it is going to stay there or not, then I can work my way back to the sermon that changed my life, and you will understand why I signed up for this course."

Peter Linden sensed that whatever he said was not going to budge the horsehair couch out of the seminar room, so he nodded to Jason Kirk to continue.

"First," said Jason, "you've got to picture Clydes Corners and my church. It's fifty miles south of here. You can take the interstate, but that will only get you within thirty miles. Then you take county road 17 west, left on Indian Mound Road and right on Preemption Road. In about five miles you'll come down a big hill with a lot of alfalfa fields and stone fences to a settlement. There are about five houses and a small store with a rusty Coca Cola sign and a clapboard church with a short-nosed steeple and big stone steps up to a stone porch outside the church's central front door. There's a wooden ramp that comes up to the stone steps from the righthand side for accessibility. I would tell you about the debate to get the ramp built, but that's nothing compared to the fight over the red horsehair couch in the chancel."

As Jason paused, Peter Linden looked down for a moment at the table and read once again the quotation printed across the top of the syllabus:

> We believe that the coming century is to witness greater triumphs in Christianity than any previous century has ever witnessed.

Peter wondered what triumph was to be announced about the red horsehair couch in Clydes Corners.

"It all started long before I came," said Jason. And then he told how Cedric Clyde, the founder of Clydes Corners, had become a successful farmer at the turn of the century. To show his thanks to God, he had paid for the building of the local Methodist church, the edifice that was still standing there in 1990. Just before Cedric died, he had donated to the church a lot of furniture for the parlor and one item for the raised chancel behind the pulpit: a giant red, horsehair couch whose rich color Cedric fancied would brighten the front of the church. The hulking object featured massive curved arms and dark mahogany legs, each carved like the claw of a lion. If any strangers who knew nothing about the faith had entered that sanctuary, they would have concluded that the central religious symbol of Christianity was not the small brass cross on the table but the humongous couch in the chancel.

The couch had occasioned a holy war between the Clyde clan and some newer families who had moved down to the country to get their children away from the drugs that were spreading into their suburban neighborhoods. The new families had bought up foreclosed farms and built beautiful homes back in the hills. They were accustomed to fine furnishings, and they detested what they had dubbed "the Victorian Leviathan" that dominated what otherwise was a plain but handsome church, a symbol of the simpler values they hoped to reclaim by moving into the country.

But the Clydes, whose own farms had fallen on hard times during the Reagan years, looked at the couch each Sunday and fondly remembered that their great-grandfather Cedric had founded the church. Although their tractors were rusting in the front yard, at least in the house of prayer the preacher sat on Cedric's couch.

"Let me tell you about proclaiming the gospel into the twenty-first century in Clydes Corners," said Jason Kirk. "I stand in that pulpit, and over here, down to the right," Jason gestured as if he were in the pulpit at that very moment, "sits the Clyde family. All of them. And over here in the middle sit the ones who don't care, and over there, front left and back left, sit the new families. And every sentence I put in the air I see them all weighing whether it is ammunition for their side or the other side. Here I am preaching about the love of God, and everything I say is filtered through a single question: Is the pastor in favor of the red horsehair couch, or is the pastor against the red horsehair couch? I regret to say that is what preaching toward the twenty-first century in Clydes Corners has come to be."

21

By the time Jason Kirk had gotten this far in his story, the jocularity had left his voice, and the sound of his speaking matched the sadness in his eyes.

Jason said, "The Clydes talk about our church being 'at war.' That's their word, not mine. I do not like using war as a metaphor. I fought in World War II, and it was what I experienced in battle that opened me to the only hope that has kept me alive since then: my hope in Jesus Christ."

Then Jason told how his best friend on the front, his legs blown off by a land mine, had died in Jason's arms. Jason went mad with rage and grief. He ran toward the enemy line, moving entirely by instinct, and rallied his unit to victory. He came home a hero, marching with all the other heroes. But in his dreams it was not brass bands that played. It was the sound of the mine going off again and again.

"Like Katherine," Jason said, "I, too, had stopped going to church until I came back one Christmas." He interrupted his story for a moment and reflected, "Maybe hospitality ought to be the note that sounds in every preacher's voice. Welcome back all those who have stopped coming. Welcome them when they return for Christmas and Easter. Do not make them feel guilty. Maybe they are as depressed as Katherine was that Sunday after she finished her thesis. Maybe the dark hours are filled with nightmares of their best friend being blown to pieces. Do not devalue as sentimental their affection for the old carols and hymns. It may be the only time in the year when they dare to let themselves feel anything at all. If there is the slightest seed of hope or faith or grace springing up in their hearts, do not stomp on it. Welcome them home.

"That is what happened to me," said Jason, "when I, like Katherine, returned to church during the Christmas season, mostly to please my folks and because I knew there would be more music than talking."

Jason's eyes glanced toward Katherine. He looked at her with an understanding that his face had not evinced when she told her story. It was not as though his story was more important than hers. There was not a shred of arrogance in his voice. It was, instead, as though the memory of his reclaimed faith had opened him to the truth of Katherine's own struggle.

Observing the change in Jason, Peter Linden wondered: "How

22

can the pulpit awaken this kind of openness to one another in the congregation?" One principle began to emerge in Peter's mind: Preaching toward the twenty-first century would have to make clear the experiences that nurture particular understandings of the gospel. Without this, Katherine and Jason might have been reduced to arguing the merits of their theology as disembodied abstractions. They might have gotten into an angry fight, while the experiential sources of their passion remained hidden.

Katherine, sensing the shift in Jason's tone, was the one who asked: "And Jason, what happened in church, when you went back that Christmas after the war? Why was the sermon so effective?"

"Well," said Jason, coming back to his story. "It was a sermon on Isaiah 11, the peaceable kingdom passage about the wolf and the lamb, the one that ends: 'They shall not hurt nor destroy in all my holy mountain: for the earth shall be full of the knowledge of the Lord, as the waters cover the sea.'

"I cannot recall the details of what the preacher said, but the memory of the sound of his voice is as clear in my head now as when I first heard it. There was a confidence, a conviction in the voice, an assurance that seemed to have come from some source nothing could ever blow away. God seemed high and mighty and safe, and I wanted to hide myself there: 'Rock of ages cleft for me, let me hide myself in thee.'

"It was that same hope that made the theology of Karl Barth so attractive to me when I went to seminary in 1950, in the middle of this century. I recall in our homiletics class we had to read *The Word of God and the Word of Man*.[1] There is a scene in the book where the church bells are ringing and the people are gathering, and Barth considers what they want to hear from the preacher. He says they want to hear a word from God, a word that will address their lives and yet in some way be a word beyond their lives, not distorted by their human limitations. At least that is the way I remember the theology in my own mind, that is the way it guided the early years of my preaching.

"I don't know if my congregations got Barth's theology right or not. I'm not sure I did. But my listeners used to say that I inspired faith because of my fervor. I wanted to proclaim this high and mighty God with such unyielding belief that the hardest, meanest heart in the world would melt before the holy word. And then at last, no one would hurt or destroy again, and earth would 'be full of the knowledge of God as the waters that cover the sea.' "

Jason's voice rose up as he spoke. Peter Linden could picture Jason Kirk as a young man in the pulpit, who had overcome the jitters of his first sermons so that his conviction was now more evident in his delivery, and listeners could sense the fire in his bones.

For that moment in class even Jason's sad eyes seemed to brighten at the echo of youthful fervor in his voice. He concluded by saying that he had signed up for "Preachers in Search of Their Voices" to feel again the passion for God's word that first led him to the pulpit. He loved that passage in Acts 20 that describes the apostle Paul "hastening to be at Jerusalem, if possible, on the day of Pentecost." Jason took the verse to mean that preachers, and indeed the entire church, needed to return to the fire that first warmed their hearts. For Jason that was the way to find one's voice for preaching into the twenty-first century: "return to the fire."

"Which fire?" asked Dorian White Elk.

"Why, the fire of the Spirit, the gift of Pentecost!" answered Jason Kirk, as though he could not imagine a preacher's not knowing which fire he meant.

"But there are many tongues of flame to the one fire," said Dorian White Elk, "and from your story I am not sure that you warm yourself at the same flame I do."

Peter recalled that the class list from the dean's office had included a Dorian White. But in the course of the semester Dorian revealed that among his people, the Comanches, he was known as White Elk. When his family moved from the reservation, his mother registered him at school as Dorian White because she thought it would make things easier for him.

Dorian White Elk was in his early fifties. His soft-spoken voice surprised Peter the first time he heard it because Peter had expected a much louder sound from this man with broad shoulders and a large barreled torso.

Although Dorian was speaking of flame and fire, his voice had none of the passion Peter usually associated with such imagery. The entire class had to sit very still whenever Dorian spoke, for even in the pulpit Dorian did not raise his voice. His people did not consider that appropriate for sacred speech.

Dorian explained that for preachers to find an effective voice for the twenty-first century they would have to listen to the gospel in new ways. Just as his people had listened to the missionaries at the end of the nineteenth century, now it was time for the white church to listen to the gospel returning to them through a people who heard God in the wind.

Peter recalled that before Dorian preached his first sermon in class, he played an Indian wooden flute to prepare them to listen with the intensity that his soft speech required.

Sitting in his green leather chair in his office, ten years later, Peter could still faintly hear the plaintive sound of Dorian's flute.

The tones drifting through his head clarified Peter's mind, and he could hear Dorian explaining that Jason and he did not warm themselves by the same flame of the Spirit.

Dorian's conversation never seemed to head in a straight line, to Peter's way of thinking. But Peter made an effort to register every word the man said, trying to understand not only the substance of Dorian's talk but also the way he spun his thoughts together. It was as though Dorian was using language to trace a web of meaning that Peter had never seen.

"I heard every word of your story," Dorian said to Jason, "but I'm not sure that you did."

"What do you mean? I spoke the words."

"Yes, but speaking words is not the same as hearing how they sound to our listeners. When you gave your directions on how to get to your church—'South on the interstate, right on county road 17, then left on Indian Mound Road'—I stopped right there: Indian Mound Road. I kept listening, but all through your story, I was thinking: Are there Indian mounds south of here? I don't come from this part of the country, so I wondered: Are there Indian mounds down toward your church?"

"Well, a long time ago there were," said Jason, "until the county leveled them to put in the road. Cedric Clyde was responsible for that, too. At least, that is what I heard. He had a lot of power with the county board of supervisors, and he had that road put in where he did because it was most convenient for taking produce back out to the old state highway. I don't suppose he thought anything at all about plowing down those mounds."

Dorian grew very still. It was a stillness that filled the room so completely that no one spoke. Then Dorian began to explain the connections in his mind between the Indian mounds, the red horsehair couch, Karl Barth, the flames of Pentecost, and finding one's voice to preach the gospel into the twenty-first century.

Trying to recall his explanation ten years after the course, Peter was sure that he was missing some of the links. But it went something like this:

Dorian said that although tribal cultures varied greatly, and although it was impossible to lump their beliefs together into one creed, nearly all American Indians honored their ancestors. Their burial grounds were sacred, and so the seemingly incidental direction 'left on Indian Mound Road,' had drawn Dorian into Jason's story more than anything else. It had provided the framework for listening to the entire story. Dorian heard it as a tale of white people fighting over whose tribe would be honored, the ancestral tribe of the Clydes, symbolized by the couch, or the invading tribe of the former suburbanites, who were displacing the natives by buying out their foreclosed farms. To Dorian it seemed like a recapitulation of what had happened to tribe after tribe as they were displaced by white settlers.

As Dorian explained how he saw things, Jason Kirk muttered, "I never thought of it like that."

Dorian said: "I think your image of God as high and mighty and safe keeps you from seeing what is actually happening. That vision of God was the flame that warmed you as a young preacher. And I can see why; it met the need of your soul after the war. But there are other tongues of flame to the Spirit's fire. Sometimes people feel them in the presence of a burial mound or even through a red horsehair couch that links them to an ancestor, who, at least in their minds, links them to God."

Now that Dorian had learned that the Indian mounds had been leveled for a road, he had yet another reading of Jason's story. It was a parable of the white church: fighting over Cedric's red couch, but never considering how Cedric's road had desecrated the sacred burial mounds of the Indians.

Dorian said, "This is the task of proclaiming the gospel into the twenty-first century: to raise from oblivion the people who have been plowed over."

Someone asked if that were the kind of sermon Dorian had written down in response to the exercise.

Dorian looked down at his paper on the table and read again the first question:

What is your best memory of a sermon or preacher that had a positive impact on your life?

He had written down nothing for an answer, and now the whole class could see from his face that he was dismantling the question inside his head and reassembling it in a way that would make more sense to him. Then he began again in his usual quiet voice. "I'm not sure I think of single sermons when I think of preaching. Of course, there were individual sermons I heard growing up, but I can recall no special one that had the impact Katherine and Jason remember. Their stories make me think of winter weather on the plains: the wind is driving snow into your face, your hands are blue with cold, you are far out from home, and you might freeze to death. Then a south wind comes up, and you can feel the frost melting on your eyebrows. You remember that kind of change. You were desperate; then you were saved.

"But most weather is not like that. And neither are most sermons. They are more like the rain. A shower waters the land. You look out and the fields are greener, but the line of the hills is the same against the sky. Yet over the years the landscape is being reshaped. Preaching is like that. Although this or that sermon brings a burst of new growth in the heart, the enduring effects of preaching take place gradually over time.

"Like the rain, much of the preaching I heard nurtured new life. Jesus became my friend, and I followed him.

"But, also like the rain, the preaching I heard caused much destruction, sweeping away my people's traditions and eroding their confidence in the wisdom of their culture. Sermon after sermon said that we could not continue our customs if we wanted to be Christian.

"It is significant to me that I am taking this course in 1990, because it was in 1893, nearly a hundred years ago, that some of my people first converted to Christianity, about when this man wrote these words." Dorian pointed to the top of the syllabus and read the quotation to the class:

We believe that the coming century is to witness greater triumphs in Christianity than any previous century has ever witnessed, and that it is to be more truly Christian than any of its predecessors.

"I was interested when Katherine pointed to the photographs on the walls. If I could have a part in refurnishing this homiletics room, I would like to add some of the photographs that my folks passed on to me. The earliest ones feature my ancestors wearing a plains feather bonnet. But the later shots show the men in formal black coats looking just like these early seminary graduates. Matter of fact, some of the missionaries were from this school. They came out and dressed us up like themselves. When we became Christian we had to give up all our Indian clothing, we had to be as white as we could be.

"When I went off to college I had a friend who asked me: 'Why do Indians dance? Why do they wear headdresses?' He meant no harm or prejudice. He was just interested. I had to tell him that I did not know. But I went home and started asking the elders about this and about that and getting straight what the old traditions and rituals were and what they meant.

"It was then I realized that preaching had done my people harm as well as good. The preaching I grew up with was like acid rain. It was giving life and corroding life at the same time. If we are going to preach the gospel into the twenty-first century, we need to purify the rain, to cleanse our preaching voices from the acids of prejudice and superiority that have poisoned preaching in the past.

"Exactly how to do this, I do not know. I only know that it will be very difficult because there are Indian Christians whose families made a huge sacrifice by joining the church. They turned their backs on the old ways in the face of strong opposition from many tribal leaders. The families of those early converts believe that to reclaim the native traditions would be to dishonor their ancestors who gave up so much to be converted."

Peter Linden was listening to Dorian, but from the corner of his eyes he was aware of the other students gathered around the table and beyond them the gallery of photographs of preachers from earlier generations.

Peter calculated that if he multiplied all of the graduates whose photographs hung on the wall by the number of sermons they each had preached throughout their ministries, the total would be in the thousands. Had it mattered that, Sunday after Sunday, they had gotten out of bed to pray and to get down to church early, and that they had often rearranged a sermon's opening paragraph for the fifth time just before they went in to lead the service?

What harm and what good had all of their preaching done?

Had all of those thousands of sermons produced some fruit of faith, some community of peace and justice, some reconciling word, some hope that saved a desperate life, some decision to give oneself entirely to the love and service of God?

Peter imagined for a moment that those early graduates were taking in every word. And then he imagined a hundred years into the future. A photograph of all the members of "Preachers in Search of Their Voices" was on the wall, and a seminar of preachers was meeting and talking about the legacy of preaching that they had inherited.

Peter felt simultaneously burdened down and lifted up. The burden was the weight of the past and all the harm that preaching had done. The lifting up was the witness of the past to the glory of God and all the good that preaching had accomplished. And feeling both burdened and lifted at the same time, Peter caught the full measure of sorrow and hope that sounded in Dorian White Elk as he finished speaking.

"But not all Indian Christians are opposed to the old ways. There are those, like myself, who want to bring into the same circle our ancient tribal traditions and the gospel, while still others will have nothing to do with Christianity because of what it has done to us in the past. The wind blows in many directions at once. I suppose that is why I signed up for 'Preachers in Search of Their Voices' because I wonder what kind of preaching can hold my people together when things fall apart."

At Dorian's concluding words, "when things fall apart," the class nearly fell apart as they all spoke at once, describing how their world and their churches were falling apart. When the class quieted down, Dorian said to Roger Hawkins, who was seated next to him, "Tell them what you were just saying."

Every face turned toward Roger Hawkins. Senior pastor of a church in the upscale suburb of Grafton Heights, Roger was a tall lanky man with dark blue eyes that matched the pin-striped suits he usually wore to class. That first day of class Roger was on crutches because he had sprained his ankle playing squash with one of the church trustees at the Y. He had joked with the class

29

when he entered the room, saying, "The old body ain't what it used to be."

But there was no levity in his voice as he responded to Dorian and explained to the whole class how things were falling apart in Grafton Heights. Although every house looked as trim and neat as the set for a standard television sitcom, in truth everything was in pieces. His people's lives were fragmented by an endless scramble to make more, own more, do more.

Roger had heard Jason's story with completely different ears from Dorian's.

When Jason had described the families moving to Clydes Corners from the suburbs, Roger had nodded his head in understanding, as if he were personally acquainted with the new members of Jason's church. Now he explained what he had been thinking.

"Those new families in the country could very well have moved from Grafton Heights. Many people in my church dream of an idyllic retreat. It is why they buy second homes in the mountains or move to a place like Clydes Corners. And when it turns out not to be the way they imagined, they try to reduce it to a problem with a tangible solution—like getting rid of the red horsehair couch. They neaten up the chancel, only to find their souls are as hungry as ever.

"I remember a few years ago, when I took another course here at the seminary. It was in systematics, on the doctrine of humanity. I was desperate to understand how people could have so much and be so empty. We were reading Reinhold Niebuhr's *The Nature and Destiny of Man,* and I came upon words that leapt from the page. They said something like this: 'The rich man always wants more riches, the husband married to a beautiful wife wants one more beautiful, the great landowner seeks to add yet another field to his estate.' And then it said, and I am certain these are the exact words: 'This incessant pursuit of an ever fugitive satisfaction springs from troubled deeps in human nature.'[5]

"Those scant words are one of the two sermons that stand out in my life. The other was not from a book. It was a sermon I heard preached when we were taking the children on a tour of historic sites and parks. We found ourselves one warm Sunday morning driving through a suburb like Grafton Heights. We stopped to go to church. As we entered, the first thing we saw in the narthex was a large poster announcing the Crafts Bazaar and Strawberry Social. Alice says to me: 'Are we pulling a camper behind us or the Grafton Heights congregation?' They even sang the same hymns at the same tempo.

"Perhaps because it seemed a mirror reflection of the church I serve, and perhaps because the preacher was about my age and build, the whole service gave me the uncanny feeling of looking in on myself leading Sunday worship. But all this changed with the sermon. I always begin with the biblical text, but this preacher did not speak about the Bible until the very end.

"Instead, he starts telling us about his vacation that was just over. He had spent some time in the city and had seen a play entitled *That Championship Season*.[6] At first I began to wonder when he was going to bring in the Bible, but after a few minutes I did not worry anymore because I found myself completely caught up in the sermon, and I could tell the whole congregation was with him.[7] You did not hear the rustling of a single bulletin.

"The play is about a basketball team that had won the state championship twenty years earlier. The plot hooked me because I was center on my high school team when I was growing up. In the play, four of the starters and the coach get together on the anniversary of the championship game. They listen to a recording of the radio broadcast and celebrate the victory once again.

"But it turns out that they cheated to win. A black player on the other team was dominating the game, so they deliberately tripped him to put him out of commission. The fifth starter on the team, the one who never returns for the anniversary celebration, later went to the coach and asked him to confess their dirty play and to return the trophy. But the coach never did. He and the others keep up the myth that they are the greatest.

"Their careers have subsequently followed the pattern of that game: win at all costs. They never allow integrity or decency or compassion to get in the way of what they want. The lurid details of their adult lives keep seeping out as the play continues. But in the final scene, they cannot face up to the truth. They gather around the old trophy and sing the school song and hang on to the lie.

"I remember sitting there in the pew, realizing I had never

listened to a sermon so intensely in my life. And then I wondered: But is it a sermon? Where is the gospel? And just as I was asking this, just as my heart and mind were thirsting for some redemptive possibility the play never offers, just then the preacher moves aside his notes and finds his place in the pulpit Bible. I wonder: What is he going to read?

"I look to the left and right in the pews around me. Every face I see appears to be saying: 'There has got to be more. Something from God. Tell us.' The preacher reads in a calm voice at a slow speed: 'What does it profit them if they gain the whole world, but lose or forfeit themselves? Let whoever has ears to hear, hear.' "

Roger Hawkins looked off in the distance, and the class could see that in telling about the sermon he was hearing it once more in his heart. He came back from his reverie, observing, "So the two most memorable sermons I ever heard were unlike anything I learned in homiletics. One was a revelatory phrase from a volume of systematic theology: 'This incessant pursuit of an ever fugitive satisfaction springs from troubled deeps in human nature.' And the other sermon was the retelling of a Broadway play with no Scripture until the last two sentences, which I received as someone dying from thirst receives a drink of water.

"I do not know if they meet your ideas of a sermon, but they were sermons for me because they worked upon me in the same way that all good sermons do. They are like lightning at night: For a second you can see everything so that you remember the shape of the land even when the dark returns. You still walk in shadow, but you have a clearer sense of where the path lies. You are able to stay more in the center of the path as you go.

"That's why I signed up for 'Preachers in Search of Their Voices,' because I want my preaching to help my people find the center."

Then Roger Hawkins turned to Katherine and said, "You taught college English. Isn't there some famous poem about everything coming apart and the center giving way? It was required reading when I took an intro course to modern literature in college."

"Yeats. 'The Second Coming,' " Katherine said. "I can't quote the whole thing, but I remember the lines I think you mean:

> Things fall apart; the center cannot hold;
> Mere anarchy is loosed upon the world,

The blood-dimmed tide is loosed, and everywhere
The ceremony of innocence is drowned;
The best lack all conviction, while the worst
Are full of passionate intensity.

"That's the poem," said Roger. "Anarchy 'loosed upon the world.' I see it behind the manicured lawns and the well-trimmed hedges of Grafton Heights. I drive by those places and think of a woman whose husband beat her up last week after they gave a cocktail party. I see another couple, the woman crying, the man's face a stone. Their son has been busted for his part in a crack ring. I listen to members of my congregation with six-figure incomes who cannot afford a pledge of more than 2 percent because of the mortgage on their second home. I see the town meeting last month and the people shouting down the supervisor who had sponsored a group home in Grafton Heights. Yes, 'the ceremony of innocence'—I had forgotten that phrase—'the ceremony of innocence is drowned' in my people's broken lives. 'Things fall apart; the center cannot hold.' As I said, that's why I'm here to figure out how to regain the center."

For a moment the members of the class were busy writing notes, asking Katherine to repeat the lines from the poem and getting the name of the play from Roger.

While the students wrote, Peter became aware of the ticking of the oak framed wall clock that had been saved from the old seminary, reconditioned and hung along with the historic photographs of the campus and its early graduates. The gentle tick-tock almost seemed to emanate from the picture of the granite Victorian building that had dominated the old campus. It was as if the past were holding on to the present by the faintest possible pulse, and only by the deliberate act of rewinding it once a week did the thing keep beating. Is that what preaching would become, rewinding the old ecclesiastical clock to soften the present with an antique sound? Would the voices of preachers be as dated as that old relic? Or would proclaiming the gospel into the twenty-first century bring wind, bring fire?

While the students wrote, Peter found himself praying the words of a hymn from the church's new hymnal while his heart filled with the sound of the music:

33

Wind who makes all winds that blow,
Gusts that bend the sapling low,
Gales that heave the sea in waves,
Stirrings in the mind's deep caves:
Aim your breath with steady power
On your church, this day, this hour.
Raise, renew the life we've lost,
Spirit God of Pentecost.[8]

Suddenly Peter realized that everyone had finished writing and he was staring at the Roman numerals on the clock's round face, admiring its large brass hands. "Two fifty!" exclaimed Peter. Class would be over in ten minutes. He apologized that they had not had time to hear everyone's story.

Looking around the room, Peter was aware that with the exception of Katherine Carr, men had done the talking. He thought of a book on the class reading list, *You Just Don't Understand: Women and Men in Conversation.* The author, Deborah Tannen, a professor of sociolinguistics, explained how women for the most part have been trained to allow a decent pause before joining in a conversation, whereas men plunge right in, assuming women will do the same.[9]

Peter remembered Katherine's saying that church had felt to her like being a daughter in a household where the men did all the talking and the women were never listened to, and he wondered whether this would happen in "Preachers in Search of Their Voices." Would the men dominate and the women not be heard? He was about to raise the issue when Tashika Bronson spoke up.

"I see from the syllabus that we're supposed to begin preaching in class next week. I'm willing to go first, but I think we should put it off until we hear everyone else's story. I believe," said Tashika, "it would be more in keeping with the understanding of preaching that I found in one of the books for this course."

Peter wondered if she meant *You Just Don't Understand: Women and Men in Conversation.* One of the themes of the book was how women tend to draw personal experience and examples into public talk, to establish a sense of connectedness in the group. Perhaps the growing number of women clergy would lead preaching in the twenty-first century to reclaim its ancient conversational roots. Perhaps sermons would feel less like finished orations and more like sharing stories and experiences around a community circle. Perhaps the voices of preachers would be more personal than the male-dominated rhetoric of the past.[10]

Tashika Bronson bent down to her book bag and brought out Fred Craddock's book *Preaching.*

"Give me a minute, and I'll find it. I marked the passage."

Tashika was a city pastor, ten years out of seminary, now returning to work on her D.Min. Her thesis topic was "Blood as an Empowering Image in the Song and Preaching of the Black Church." Tashika was a slender, petite woman whose eyes shone with such intensity that listeners felt she was seeing to the bottom of their souls, even if they were sitting all the way back in the last pew.

"Here it is," she said, reading from a section on the vital contribution of listeners to sermons:

> Sermons should speak *for* as well as *to* the congregation. . . If a minister takes seriously the role of listeners in preaching . . . [they will] say, "Yes, that is my message; that is what I have wanted to say." All of us recognize here a dynamic that has long been operative in many black churches but which has been absent in traditions in which preachers only speak to but not in and for the faithful community.[11]

Tashika scanned the entire group with her eyes of laser intensity. Then pointing to the book in her hands, she asked: "How are we going to preach like this? How are we going to take seriously the role of the listeners in this class unless we hear everyone's story? Look how different we are. Our stories are revealing the world that each of us brings to this course."

Then Tashika, sensing that she was introducing herself in her own way to the class, went to the blackboard and drew a cloud, printing the word *God* inside it. Next she drew a straight arrow downward to a vertical rectangle where she printed: "Pulpit and Preacher." And finally beneath the pulpit she drew another arrow to a large square with the word *congregation.* All of this was done with bold lines and big block print. Its simplicity and giant size gave the diagram a visual strength that dominated the room.

Looking at it one could feel the word of God rushing from heaven right through the preacher and into the congregation with the force of an iron meteor falling from the sky.

"This model of preaching will not work for this class," said Tashika. "Just think of how many different subtle ways God has spoken in the stories we have heard today."

"Yes," said Jason, "But Clydes Corners is not like this class. There are the couch lovers and the couch haters, but not this much variety in my congregation. This is not the real world."

"Who defines what the real world is for a preacher?" asked Tashika. "For a preacher the real world is the whole world, or as much of the whole world as a preacher can grasp. God wants to redeem more than just your little corner or my little corner. God wants the whole thing saved, the world in which the women have been ignored and the land mine has blown our best friend to pieces and the family farms have been foreclosed and the Indian mounds plowed over and the tribal customs suppressed and the championship season purchased at the cost of the players' souls and the wife beaten after the cocktail party. If we know only a tiny part of that world, and if our people know only a tiny part of that world, then it's our job as preachers to tell them about the other parts.

"The other day I was reading from a collection of writings by radical women of color, *This Bridge Called My Back*. A woman named Cherrie Moraga says, 'What each of us needs to do about what we don't know is to go look for it.'[12] That is what we have been doing here today: We have been looking at what we don't know about one another's world. We need to look for what we don't know so we can be faithful to God. We need to look for what we don't know so we can be compassionate to one another. We need to look for what we don't know so that we can understand why there are so many different voices for proclaiming the gospel."

Tashika moved to the next slate of blackboard and drew a circle as wide in diameter as her first diagram was high. It filled the whole slate. She said: "I got the idea for this from Craddock's words, but I'm developing it in my own way." Then she started drawing lines from the center to the rim and putting arrow points headed in and out on each line. Tashika explained that everyone was in the circle, but sometimes one of them would move to the center of the circle, as when they listened in turn to Katherine, Jason, Dorian, and Roger. When they were in the center, they were to share the special gift they had, but always remembering what it was like for the others in the circle. No one was to dominate the center, but to use it as the holy privilege that it was.

"If we acted like this throughout the course we would not just talk past one another," Tashika said. "We would hear each other, and we would learn amazing things. And if we went home and preached like this, God's word might be identified in ways we never dreamed possible."

Ten years later, sitting in his office chair with the cracked green leather seat, Peter continued to study Tashika's diagrams in his mind's eye. Suddenly there was a knock at the office door, and Peter looked up, noticing the calendar: **January 2000.**

Then he looked at his watch and remembered he had an appointment with a student who was getting ready to preach his first sermon.

Peter said, "Be there in a minute." He got up and stretched his legs. He almost wished he had not taken out the class list for "Preachers in Search of Their Voices" because now the students from the course were so vividly present in his office that he could not ask them to leave. He found himself saying to them out loud, "I'll get back to you in a little while."

Hearing Peter's voice through the door, the student out in the hall said, "If you have someone with you, I'll come back later."

"No, come in, come in," said Peter opening the door.

The student was an earnest young man, very anxious about getting into the pulpit for the first time. He sat down and said: "I know nothing about preaching sermons except that I've heard a lot of them. So where do I begin?"

Peter said: "By remembering what it's like to stand on the rim of the circle, not at the center."

"What?" asked the baffled student. "Are you describing some method of sermon construction?"

"Yes, in a way it is a method, but it is also more than that. You might call it a posture for the preacher's soul. It's something I learned from a student on the opening day of a course about finding our voices as preachers."

Chapter 2

Neglected Voices

Listening to Outsiders

It was quiet once again in Peter Linden's office. The student who had sought help preparing his first sermon was gone. Peter glanced at the new calendar on the wall: **January 2000.** Then he looked at the old class list and returned to his memories of "Preachers in Search of Their Voices."

Peter recalled entering the seminar room for the second meeting of class. No one had erased Tashika Bronson's diagrams. God was still in the cloud rushing down through the pulpit into the congregation.

The vertical axis of God's descent stood in contrast to the one beside it: the circle with arrows moving back and forth between the center and the rim.

Peter looked from one diagram to the other. Before his eyes stood two different ways of understanding preaching: Jason Kirk's mighty God coming down from on high and Tashika Bronson's dynamic circle. Peter was just about to erase the board as students started coming in the door, and behind his back he heard someone say, "Leave those up, please."

Peter turned around to see Marjorie Hudson pointing at the board. "I was hoping no one erased them. It wasn't until Tashika drew them that I remembered the sermon that had the greatest influence on me."

Like many seminarians of the late twentieth century, Marjorie Hudson was a second-career student. She was a tall woman whose gray hair was pulled back in a bun, giving the impression that she was about to attack a strenuous job and did not want anything to get in her way. When she looked at people, her steel blue eyes fixed directly on theirs. She had been a nurse in an inner-city hospital for over twenty-five years, most of the time as supervising nurse in the emergency room. Her size and manner were commanding enough to establish her authority when she told a patient with an earache: "You'll have to wait. They just brought someone in with a knife wound."

Marjorie told the class: "I can see now, looking back, that the sermon I most remember began on the Tuesday night before the Sunday I heard it. I know that sounds crazy, but the sermon I have in mind was more than words from the pulpit. It was a message from God that I did not realize was taking shape in me until I went to church and heard my pastor. To tell you the sermon, I have to tell you where it came from. If preachers want to be more effective, they need to understand how sermons grow in their listeners.

"Like I said, the sermon started on a Tuesday night. I was scheduled to go off duty in the emergency room at 11:30, but two nurses called in sick with the flu, and I agreed to stay into the next shift until more help was available.

"So many mothers had brought in their children with temperatures and hacking coughs that we had run out of chairs for them. To get to the rest rooms you had to step over women who were sitting on the floor with little ones in their laps.

"We were just beginning to get things under control when a man comes through the door from the emergency driveway and walks up to my desk. His arm is around a woman's shoulder, holding her up. She's wearing the man's overcoat, like a cape, her arms not in the sleeves. She's huddled down inside it with the collar turned up. I see these little eyes looking out at me, the right one all puffy underneath and dark purple.

"The man starts yelling at me, 'I want to see a doctor right away. My wife here fell down the stoop. Slipped on the ice. We came home and, well, we'd both had a little too much, and I said, "Honey, watch the top step," her being in heels and everything.' Then down she goes, landing on her cheek on those sharp steps.'

"I looked at the woman's feet. She had on sneakers. Then I looked at the man and realized the couple was from our church. I did not know them. Sundays I was up front in the choir, and they sat in the middle back, far right. I could picture them sitting in the pew with his arm up around her during the sermon, the same way it was up around her in the emergency room. If they recognized me, they pretended not to.

"The doctors had changed shifts by now, and one of them motions to me to come over. He asks me in a low voice: 'Did the woman trip on the cellar stairs with the laundry? That was the story last month.' "

Marjorie told the class how the husband kept insisting that he was to be in the room when the doctor tended his wife. The man yelled so loudly that he awakened the children sleeping in their mothers' laps, and soon the place was filled with the cries of frightened infants. But in the end Marjorie prevailed and got the woman off in a room by herself. After the doctor, Marjorie brought in a social worker who had a hotline to a shelter for battered women.

But through her bruised lips, all the woman would say was "I'll go home. I'll be all right. I just want to go home." Her voice was small and thin, and her eyes kept looking off to the distance, as though she feared looking directly at Marjorie or the social worker.

That Sunday the man and woman were in church. Marjorie was in the narthex, waiting with the choir for the processional hymn when the couple entered. Marjorie overheard one of the ushers asking the woman, who had seven stitches above the right eye, what had happened. The husband answered for her:

"Terrible fall on the stoop last Tuesday. Didn't get the ice cleared off. I could kick myself."

He sounded so convincing that Marjorie almost believed it.

"During the service," Marjorie recounted to the class, "I found myself taking quick glances at the couple. He sat there with his arm up around her, the same strong hold he used bringing her into the emergency room. I started to listen to the hymns we sang and the prayers we offered in the light of that battered woman.

" 'Almighty Father, we have sinned against you, by claiming more than is ours.' I could see the woman's lips repeating the prayer of confession. Those were not the words she needed to pray. She had not claimed too much for herself. She needed to claim more.

"Then we sang a hymn. I do not remember what it was, but every stanza reinforced that we are too filled with pride. I saw the man and the woman singing the words, her swollen lips barely parting, as she mouthed a hymn of contrition.

"And then there was the sermon. I remember the text the preacher used because it is so well known—the passage in 2 Corinthians that begins 'If anyone is in Christ he is a new creation.' It goes on to say that 'in Christ God was reconciling the world to himself, not counting their trespasses against them, and entrusting to us the message of reconciliation.'

"I can tell you the sermon in one sentence: Since God did not count our trespasses against us, we must not count our trespasses against each other. The preacher painted visions of what might happen if wives and husbands, neighbors and nations would only forgive each other.

"I glanced at the woman and her husband. She had the same distant look in her eyes that she had in front of the social worker and me at the hospital. But her husband was listening attentively to the preacher. There was nothing in his face that would give away the events of the last week.

"Listening to the sermon and seeing the couple became agony for me. I tried to look away. I tried to reassure myself that the sermon was true for other people, if not for the woman. I tried looking down at my lap to block the preacher from my sight, but my eyes fell again on the prayer of confession: 'Almighty Father, we have sinned against you, by claiming more than is ours.' I began to choke on the words of the prayer and the sermon. I thought I would have to get up and leave, but to do that I would have to walk across the chancel since there was no door on the choir side.

"Then I started thinking: If I were to preach a sermon on behalf of this battered woman, what would I say? With the help of Tashika's diagrams, I can now see why I was so frustrated. The preacher was speaking words as if they had rushed out of the clouds, out of heaven to earth, as if they were universally true when they were not. The preacher said things like, 'We all must forgive people no matter what they do to us.' But the only thing a cheap pardon purchases from an abuser is more violence. I knew that as a nurse, not as a theologian. This week, however, I started a book on our reading list that gave me new words for what I was feeling in church that Sunday."

Marjorie reached into her tapestry shoulder bag and brought out Elisabeth Schüssler Fiorenza's *Bread Not Stone: The Challenge of Feminist Biblical Interpretation.* "Here is the sentence I underlined," she said. " 'While feminist theology advocates for men a "theology of relinquishment," it articulates for women a theology of "self-affirmation." '[1]

"The sermon I heard while I was observing the abused woman from the choir featured a theology of relinquishment. The preacher assumed throughout that his listeners were powerful enough, confident enough in themselves to be gracious. But the battered woman had no sense of self-power. Or if she did, she dared not show her self-power because her husband would crush her, perhaps even murder her. It happens. I've seen the bodies.

"That morning, sitting in the choir, I had no terms for describing my discomfort. My vocabulary of salvation was limited to the hymns, the prayers, and the preaching I had grown up with, and I can see now that it was overwhelmingly a theology of relinquishment. I had no knowledge of a theology of self-affirmation.

"All I knew was that I wanted to preach a sermon to reverse the impact of the sermon I was hearing. I wanted a sermon that would confront the abuser with the evil he was doing, that would get him to stop and never do it again.

"There he sat, taking in the sermon as a devout believer. My years of nursing had taught me enough psychology to know that in his mind he was no hypocrite. It all made sense to him: beating his wife, covering it up, coming to church, praying 'Almighty Father,' singing the hymn of contrition, and listening to the sermon. That morning I realized as never before how a sermon may reinforce the structures of abuse, even if that is not the preacher's intention. This is why I signed up for 'Preachers in Search of Their Voices,' because I want to preach a faith in Jesus Christ that can never, never be used as a rationalization for violence.[2]

"So there I am in the choir, trying to figure out a sermon to counter the one I'm hearing. I bet a lot of sermons we preach into the twenty-first century will be like that, sermons to counter the sermons of the past. Jesus preached that way: 'You have heard it said . . . but I say to you. . . . '

"At any rate, I sit there in the choir and start thinking about the Bible. I had grown up in the church, and I was there just about every Sunday because I sang in the choir, but I was no big Bible reader. And to tell the truth, the music often seemed to bring me closer to God than the Scripture. But I give it a try anyway, and I

42

ask myself if there is some story about a battered woman in the Bible. But the only women whose names come quickly to mind are Eve, Sarah, Bathsheba, Ruth, Mary, and Martha. I know there are more than that, but they are the ones I could recall having heard a lot about.

"Keeping that battered woman in mind, I thought of what I knew about each one of the biblical women I remembered. Eve gets blamed for tempting Adam. Sarah has a child after menopause. David takes out his lust on Bathsheba. Ruth and Mary sound too good to be true. And as for Martha, I always hated how she got dumped on for worrying about the meal. My memory of women in the Bible left me with nothing to say to the battered woman in the pew.

"Remember, this is before I went to seminary. I had no idea of books like Fiorenza's or that feminist lectionary you have on the reading list.[3] I am describing how I thought about the Bible back then. If you want to proclaim the gospel into the twenty-first century, you have to deal with more than what is on the page of Scripture. You have to deal with people's ideas about the Bible. Many of those ideas do not come from the Bible itself. They come from sermons, hymns, prayers, and thoughts that float around in the culture: like Christmas cards and table grace at sports banquets and invocations on Veterans Day. You could preach a thousand perfect sermons, but if you never dealt with what listeners already think about the Bible in their heads, at the end of all those sermons, they would still be thinking the same thing.[4]

"What I am telling you is this: After all my years of listening to sermons, when I tried to come up with a sermon for this battered woman, the Bible did not seem to be any help."

"So how did you figure out a sermon for the battered woman?" asked Jason Kirk, the pastor from Clydes Corners.

"I gave up on the Bible and concentrated instead on the woman's experience, the hell she was living in."

"I understand concentrating on the woman's experience," said Jason, "but I can't imagine a sermon without the Bible."

"I can't imagine a sermon without God," responded Marjorie with fire in her voice. "Before there was a Bible, there was God. If we can't find in the Bible what we need for a sermon, the Bible teaches God is loving enough to help us find it somewhere else. That is what I like best about the Bible; it is not as limited as the people who want to limit God to the Bible. The Bible keeps pointing beyond itself to stars, to mountains, to rivers, to wind and flame, to Jesus, who won't stay put between the covers of any book. So if you want to be biblical you have to get outside the Bible in the same way the Bible gets outside itself.

"Like I said, I put the Bible aside and focused on the woman's experience. Then I asked myself what I dreamed for her. I pictured her with the stitches out, with the bruise gone from her cheek, and her lips no longer puffy. I imagined her speaking in a clear, confident voice. I imagined beauty shining in her eyes. I did not have in mind the slick beauty of magazine covers, but the beauty that fills the faces of children when they learn to ride a bicycle on their own, the beauty of knowing you can balance and pedal and turn on your own, the beauty of being 'a new creation'! The phrase leapt into my mind from the reading, 'If anyone is in Christ, they are a new creation.' "

"So you did come back to the Bible," Jason observed with relief in his voice.

" 'Back to the Bible' is not how I would put the matter," said Marjorie. "That sounds too much like I imposed the Bible on the woman, like the husband imposing his strength on her. If nothing in the Bible confirmed it, I still would have preached my dream for the woman. I knew that dream was from God."

"But you knew it," said Isaiah Thompson, "because your dream matched the dreams in the Bible."

"Not necessarily," Marjorie replied. "The Bible has often been used to suppress the holy dreams of the human heart. There are terrible as well as beautiful things in the Bible. No one preaching into the twenty-first century can afford to forget that people use the Bible to justify atrocities as well as to march for justice."

Marjorie reopened Schüssler Fiorenza's book *Bread Not Stone,* the same book that earlier had given her the terms "a theology of relinquishment" and a "theology of self-affirmation." She said, "Here, listen to this:

'The history of the church and its appeal to the authority of Scripture shows that biblical traditions are not only life giving but also death dealing. The appeal to Scripture has authorized, for example, the persecution of Jews, the burning of witches, the torture of heretics, national wars in Europe, the subhuman conditions of American slavery, and the antisocial politics of the Moral Majority.' "[5]

While Marjorie was reading the quotation, Isaiah Thompson's face clouded with the sadness that fills any of us when we realize the flaws in someone we love. "Yes," he said, "that is true about the Bible and true about the way it has been used. But you must remember that the Bible that was used to shackle the slaves is the Bible that was used to free the slaves."

Isaiah Thompson looked much taller than his average height because of his straight posture and the dignity with which he carried himself. Isaiah had been well known as a gospel musician before he went to seminary, and years of singing solos and leading choirs had marked him with an authoritative presence, whether he was standing in the pulpit or sitting at the seminar table.

He said, "Marjorie, you told us we need to understand how people think about the Bible, not just what is on the page, but what it stands for in their minds. Well, for me the Bible means strength, the Bible means hope, the Bible means liberation. When I was a child my mother often quoted the Bible to me. She especially loved the book of Isaiah. She named me after the prophet and often recited his words to me.

"When the electricity went off because the landlord didn't keep up on utilities, she would stand there in the dark, repeating: 'The sun shall be no more thy light by day, neither for brightness shall the moon give light unto thee: but the Lord shall be unto thee an everlasting light, and thy God thy glory.'

"When I was sick and too weak to get up, I could hear her whispering next to my bed: 'He giveth power to the faint, and to *them that have* no might he increaseth strength.'

"After my mother recited a verse, she would start humming hymns and spirituals. Sometimes I would hum with her. Sometimes we would both start singing." Isaiah Thompson looked off into the distance, and the class could see in his face that he was hearing a hymn once again in his memory:

> I want Jesus to walk with me.
> I want Jesus to walk with me.
> All along my pilgrim journey,
> Lord, I want Jesus to walk with me.[6]

45

Isaiah Thompson returned from the song and explained: "When my mother sang the great old hymns and when she quoted the Bible to me, she looked like a woman of fabulous wealth going through her store of precious stones.

"The Bible and her songs were the only riches she had. She was pregnant with me when my father went off to World War II. Like Jason's friend, he never returned.

"So there was my mother, a widowed black woman with an infant just as the war was winding down and men were returning to take back the jobs that women had held. Of course, the best jobs had gone to white women. Still, my mother had managed something pretty good on an assembly line. But when the war was over, she was let go, and she had to take to cleaning houses.

"One day she brought home a radio. The woman whose house she cleaned gave it to her because it wasn't working. The radio was the kind they used to put on mantles, an arched wooden cabinet with trellis-like grille work over the speaker.

"I came home from school and found my mother at the kitchen table unscrewing the back of the radio. She told me to get my crayons and a piece of paper and bring them to her. Then she started drawing a picture of each thing she found; if it was a red wire, she drew a red wire, if blue, then blue. She laid each piece on the table in the order she took them out. Pretty soon she had half the radio apart and a diagram on how to put the whole thing back together.

"This was in the days before solid state so a lot of what she had on the table was vacuum tubes. She studied the thing for a while, and then sent me down to the radio repair shop with two tubes and the money to buy replacements. I came back, she reassembled the thing, plugged it in, and we had music in the house!

"I remember thinking, 'My mother knows how to repair radios, but the only job they let her have is cleaning house.'

"Every morning we listened to the news after we had first read the Bible. When I learned in seminary that we ought to have the Bible in one hand and the newspaper in the other, I thought, 'My mother could have taught theology, but the only job they let her have is cleaning house.'

"Through all of this she kept preaching sermons to me, always reminding me that 'the grass withereth, the flower fadeth: but the word of our God shall stand for ever.' My mother could have been a pastor, but the only job they let her have is cleaning house."

As Isaiah Thompson spoke it was apparent from the strength in his eyes and the confidence in his voice that he had done more than memorize Bible verses. He had inherited the wealth of his mother's faith. But as Isaiah himself explained, it took a while before he claimed the riches she had given him. He first had some growing up to do.

"When I went off to college, I was eager to appear sophisticated, and I was embarrassed by my mother's faith. When students in the dorm asked me about my family, I told about my mother repairing the broken radio and how she had earned a reputation in the apartment building for being able to fix anything, clocks, stoves, toasters, anything that was wired. I was proud of her for this, and I was glad that I had the same gift. When I told the other electrical engineering majors how my mother got me interested in the field, I could see they were impressed. So I just left things there and never told them about her religious side.

"When I graduated, the civil rights movement was beginning to make some new openings for black people in the job market. I was among the first to benefit, landing a good job as a design engineer.

"I got involved in the movement myself, partly out of personal gratitude and partly from the memory of my mother having to clean houses when she could have been repairing radios, or even designing them if she had been allowed the education that I got. It was the movement that brought me back to church.

"One night I was at a rally in a big Baptist church like the one my mother and I used to attend when I was growing up. We started singing the old songs, and I found myself drawn in by the music. If we're going to talk about proclaiming the gospel into the twenty-first century, maybe we preachers ought to give more time to the musicians. There is no telling how many people the Spirit has saved with music.

"It was music that brought me back to church. I joined the choir and pretty soon was doing solos. I still felt awkward about the faith of my childhood. I convinced myself that the reason I was going to church again was only the music, the way it filled some need I could not diagram or explain.

"At the time I was working on a project to improve color

television broadcasting. I was caught up in the technical challenge of it. Sometimes we made a breakthrough and I felt a surge of satisfaction, but it always faded quickly away. My greatest successes on the job never reached the same deep place in my soul that the music in church did.

"One Sunday we have a guest preacher, not a big name, not a star in the eyes of the media, but simply someone who knows how to preach. He announces his text and invites us to read along in our Bibles. I don't have a Bible, but I don't need one because as he begins to read I find my lips moving, reciting in a low whisper every word he speaks aloud: " 'For as the heavens are higher than the earth, so are my ways higher than your ways, and my thoughts than your thoughts.'

"It was as if some old family chest had been opened, and I was looking with new eyes at things I thought I had packed away for good:

> 'For as the rain cometh down, and the snow from heaven, and returneth not thither, but watereth the earth and maketh it bring forth and bud, that it may give seed to the sower, and bread to the eater: So shall my word be that goeth forth out of my mouth: it shall not return unto me void, but it shall accomplish that which I please, and it shall prosper *in the thing* whereto I sent it.'

"The preacher began his sermon with a reflection on the common legal phrase 'null and void.' He talked about a contract's being 'null and void' because one of the parties had violated the terms. He described how a guarantee can be 'null and void' because a customer has abused a product. Then he shifted from the law to everyday dealings with people, how someone's word to us may turn out to be null and void, how city hall may assure us there will be no more discrimination, but their policy of fair treatment turns out to be null and void.

"Then the preacher tells how he recently bought a color TV. Remember: this is when engineers like myself are just beginning to make the color reliable. The preacher brings the set home and reads the instruction booklet that begins, 'Welcome to the wonderful world of full-color television. Through the marvel of modern technology you are about to enter a new universe.' So the preacher turns on the set, and the first thing he sees is some demonstrators being driven back with fire hoses and police dogs. The 'wonderful world of full-color television,' the promise of 'a new universe' was null and void.

"I sat there in church thinking of our staff meetings back at the office, our talk about the importance of our project, how solid state technology would one day solve all our problems.

"Then the preacher began to make a turn in the sermon. You could hear the strain of it in his voice, in the way he started asking questions.

" 'Should we outlaw words because they prove null and void? Should we forbid promises of justice because they prove null and void? Should we ban the claims of liberty for all because they prove null and void? Or is there some word that is not null and void? Is there any word, anywhere, from anyone that is not null and void?'

"The preacher looked around, and the congregation's verbal responses fell off into silence. They all sensed that if they spoke now their words would be null and void. No human word would suffice to answer the preacher's question. The silence was like the silence that must have been before anything was. Then the preacher slowly and quietly began to repeat phrases out of the biblical text: 'my thoughts *are* not your thoughts, neither *are* your ways my ways, saith the Lord.' As the preacher continued to speak, his voice began to crescendo, building to the verse we were hungering for: 'So shall my word be that goeth forth out of my mouth: it shall not return unto me VOID but it shall accomplish that which I please, and it shall prosper *in the thing* whereto I sent it.'

"I do not recall exactly how the sermon ended because I was so caught up in the sense of personal revelation. I could now name the disquiet in my soul that was the true reason for my return to church: God's word had gone forth through my mother, and God's word was waiting to return to God through my own faith and life, through my acknowledgment of the truth of what she had taught me.

"So my best memory of a preacher is really a memory of two preachers: my mother and the preacher whose sermon helped me to reclaim what my mother had taught me. As a black woman, my mother had suffered more than her share of words that turned out to be null and void. She took joy in a word from heaven because there was no one higher up the line to rescind it. No one could destroy the word of God, not the government that sent my father into battle, not the boss in the factory who fired her before any white women, not the families whose houses she cleaned. They would all have to bow to God's word.

"That is why," said Isaiah Thompson, pointing to the blackboard, "my understanding of preaching is like the first diagram, the word coming down from heaven. My mother survived on that word, and I don't want to risk losing it by joining some circle where anybody at any moment will take over the center and refuse to give it up to the rest of us.

"I see now that all the time I was listening to the old radio, my mother was providing me with words and visions to understand what was being broadcast. My mother knew that you don't fix the world by fixing the radio. If you want to hear good news on that radio, you have to fix the world, and to fix the world you need something greater than the world: a word from on high. That's what preachers need into the twenty-first century: a word from on high."

Marjorie Hudson responded to Isaiah Thompson's story in a voice that revealed her heart was torn in two directions. She had been moved by the witness of Isaiah's mother, the wisdom and the faith she passed on to him.

"And yet for me," said Marjorie, "I fear a word from on high will be used to camouflage human power. I fear it will be a model of authority reinforcing the way the man made the battered woman bend to his violence. God high up and earth below implies that the world must be organized from the top down, from the powerful to the weak.

"Last year in systematics we read Sallie McFague's *Models of God*. She says that 'power as domination' is 'a central feature of the Western view of God.'[7] I fear most sermons reinforce that view. They communicate a theology of power as domination. I struggled with that sermon for the abused woman because the model of preaching I inherited assumes that power comes down from on high. Power dominates. No matter how much the preacher talked about reconciliation that Sunday, there was a different message inherent in his understanding of God. A dominating God won the attention of the abuser, while the battered woman stared off into the distance."

"But God was not reinforcing violence through my mother,"

50

said Isaiah Thompson. "God was giving strength. God was giving dignity—the very qualities you want for that battered woman."

"That's true," answered Marjorie. "But your story was powerful because of who was preaching: your mother, a widowed black woman, one who is usually forced to stand on the rim of the circle or even outside of it. She moved to the center in your story. It was not until the end of the story that you told how important it was to have the word come from on high. If you had started there, then I am not sure I would have listened so intensely. But you started with your mother, with the lights going out because the bill wasn't paid, with your being sick and her praying, with her cleaning houses. I knew I was hearing the truth. When your mother quoted from Isaiah it had authority, not because it came down from heaven, but because it illumined her experience."

Some preachers favored Marjorie Hudson's position; others favored Isaiah Thompson's. Nearly everyone got into the conversation as the class wrestled with the authority of Scripture and the authority of experience. But no one was able to settle the debate. When anyone tried to formulate a principle that would apply for all preachers and churches, there were at least two or three people who could show how that way of putting things did not fit their culture or their experience or their understanding of the Bible.

The class fell silent as the students realized there was no quick fix for their differences. The only sound in the room was the ticking of the nineteenth-century wall clock. The sound reminded Peter Linden of the earlier generations of graduates whose photographs were on the walls. Peter imagined himself a professor back in 1891, and the students, all men in stiff white shirts and black cravats, were discussing the authority of the pulpit. Whenever they came to a point of irresolvable difference, they looked to him, The Reverend Professor Doctor Peter Linden, the man who had the authority to settle the question of authority.

But Peter returned instantly to 1990, when Karen Steel suggested: "Maybe we need a new term. Maybe *authority* is not the right word any longer. In our own age, there has been so much abuse of authority that the word is suspect. I have a different term to propose. It's a word that makes sense out of our best memories of preaching."

Karen Steel was the youngest member of the class, having entered seminary straight out of college. She had a quick smile

51

and dancing eyes. The liveliness in her face gave the impression of continuous physical energy, even though her delivery in the pulpit was quite restrained.

"The word I would use instead of authority," said Karen, "comes from the sermon I most remember. Before I tell you the word, I will tell you the sermon that gave me the word. One thing I've already learned in this course is that although we spell a word with the same letters, we define it with different experiences.

"The sermon I have in mind was presented by a junior high fellowship. It was at the developmental center where I do my field education. I'm assistant to the chaplain there. We have a program of local church groups leading our Sunday afternoon worship.

"Three months ago a junior high fellowship signed up to do a service. Their advisors brought them to the center several weeks ahead of time. The chaplain and I explained the program and introduced them to some of the residents.

"Seeing those kids reminded me of when I was in junior high fellowship. The girls gathered to themselves and listened seriously to the chaplain and me. But Ed and Sue Williams, the adult advisors, had their hands full with the boys, telling them to pay attention and pulling them apart when one knuckled the other in the head.

"Some of the boys were fascinated that wherever there was a step up there was a ramp beside it. One of them had some ball bearings in his pocket, and he rolled them down the ramp to see which would go the farthest.

"I could not imagine how those junior high kids could lead our community's worship. Some of our residents are themselves hyperactive. Others use wheelchairs or walkers. Some residents can speak full sentences, but most of them are more apt to hug you or hold your hand or move their heads when they want to communicate.

"We finished our tour of the center in the gymnasium where we hold services. The chaplain asked if there were any questions. Much to my surprise the first one to raise a hand was the boy who rolled the ball bearings down the ramp.

" 'Yeah, what are those things over there?' The boy pointed to two ramps made out of hollow metal tubing, like the scaffolding contractors use. The ramps are on wheels, with a brake that keeps them from rolling once they are in place.

"The chaplain explained that the ramps could be positioned for easy access to the stage during awards ceremonies and other special programs.

" 'Can we use the ramps for our worship?' asked the boy.

"All the other kids turned toward him, and one of them said, 'You gonna roll bearings down 'em, Gerry?'

" 'Nope,' he answers. 'I got better ideas than that. People around here like ramps. We ought to do something with ramps in our worship.'

" 'Like what?' asked several of his friends.

" 'I don't know just yet. But I'm going to think of something.'

"A few weeks later the fellowship returns to lead our Sunday afternoon worship service. They arrive a full hour ahead of time, bringing with them two stacks of unmarked cardboard cartons, all of them folded flat. Gerry, the boy who had asked about the ramps, takes control and directs things, like a foreman at a construction site.

"By the time the service is to begin dozens of assembled boxes are scattered around the gymnasium. The rolling ramps are stored far away from the stage.

"The chaplain brings things to order. When she says we are going to begin worship, the group gets as quiet as it ever does. We sing a few of our favorite refrain songs, as we do with every group that visits us. That part always goes well. It is usually the readings from the Bible and the preaching that lose our residents. The readings are too long, and the sermons are too talky, so the residents get bored and start to act out their impatience. But not this Sunday.

"Gerry steps to the microphone, which is floor level. He reads in a slow voice a single Bible verse, Galatians 6:2. Meanwhile four junior high girls come out on stage and unroll a long sheet of newsprint with the Bible verse in giant block letters: 'Carry each other's burdens and so live out the law of Christ.'[8]

"Then one of the older girls steps up to the mike and starts reading a story. I later found out the plot was Gerry's, but the whole group contributed ideas, and the girl who read the story put it in final form.

"I can't remember the sermon word for word, but it was basically a parable about a church that wanted everyone to know

53

how wonderful Jesus is. They sent out invitations for everyone to come to their service.

"At this point in the sermon, two junior highs come out in tights and turtlenecks and stand at center stage, facing each other with their hands meeting and forming the front roof line of a church. You can tell it's a church because they hold up a cross where their hands meet to form the peak of the roof.

"Then the girl at the microphone resumes reading the story. She tells how the people of the church come to realize that people who use walkers and wheelchairs cannot get to the door. So they decide to build ramps.

"At this point in the story other members of the youth fellowship start picking up the empty cartons, pretending the boxes are massive building stones. The junior highs struggle to balance them on their shoulders and start to come toward the stage. But then they groan and gasp and fall down, hamming it up as only junior highs can do.

"The congregation loves it. The residents who are mobile and who like to act things out themselves get into the story. They start picking up the boxes and doing the same thing. For a minute I see complete chaos coming.

"But then the young woman begins to read again, and she startles everyone into quiet. She says in a melodramatic voice: 'The stones were too heavy for anyone to lift alone. How would they ever get the ramps built?'

"Then the four girls who are still up on stage holding the newsprint roll with the Bible verse all call out in unison: 'Carry each other's burdens and so live out the law of Christ.'

"The junior high stone masons get this super-amazed look on their faces, and they point from themselves to each other and back. Then they pair up and start lifting the boxes into place, still groaning but now managing the heavy weight. Not to be left out, the residents join in again. There are a few tense moments because it's evident that the junior highs have not foreseen this would happen, and the residents are carrying boxes all over the gymnasium. But Gerry, the ball bearing kid, whispers and motions to his friends for each of them to pair themselves with a resident, and this way every box gets put in the right place.

"At each end of the stage, they build a stepped wall of boxes, rising up from the gymnasium floor to stage level. When they roll the portable ramps into position behind the box walls you can no longer see the tubing and wheels. If you stretch your imagination, the front of the stage now looks like the front view of a church with a permanent masonry ramp on each side.

"The junior highs and staff roll the residents who are in wheel chairs onto the stage, where they are given a bright cardboard cross with the words: 'Jesus loves you.'

"Some of the residents start singing over and over again the first stanza of 'Jesus Loves Me, This I Know.' Ed Williams, the fellowship advisor, is at the piano, and he starts playing and everyone who can joins in."

> Jesus loves me! This I know,
> for the Bible tells me so.
> Little ones to him belong;
> they are weak, but he is strong.
> Yes, Jesus loves me! Yes, Jesus loves me!
> Yes, Jesus loves me! The Bible tells me so.

"They keep singing and singing," said Karen. "And all the while there is this procession of residents: up and down the ramps to receive a cross. Some of the residents who can walk go up three or four times, and every time they get a new cross. The junior highs had made loads of extras because on their introductory visit Gerry had noticed that the bulletin boards were filled with pictures and artwork, and he had said, 'They like ramps, and they like things for their walls, so we've got to make plenty of extras.' "

Karen Steel's dancing eyes slowed as she finished telling the class her story: "Several adult visitors whose family members are residents of the center came up to receive crosses as well. Many of them were crying. And several stayed afterwards to tell the junior highs, 'You will never know how much this meant to our family today.' But the junior high kids, embarrassed by such a show of emotion from the adults, stammered something back and cast their eyes to the floor."

Karen stopped and then observed: "I never thought about a sermon for so long and so hard in all my life. It was a sermon about carrying each other's burden, and it was a sermon about building ramps to a church. But it was also much more than that. Those junior highs had built a ramp to the congregation's life. They made the gospel, 'Jesus loves you,' accessible for our residents.

"Accessibility means more to me than authority.[9] The sermon Katherine heard after her thesis was finished made God accessible by removing the barrier of masculine language. The preacher that Jason remembers made God accessible through the assurance of his voice. The preacher Isaiah remembers made his mother's faith accessible to him through the story of the color television. But the preacher Marjorie remembers did not make the gospel accessible because he maintained the barrier of power as domination.

"We call Christ 'The Way' because Christ makes God accessible to us. Preaching is most Christlike when it does the same for our listeners."

"Listeners?" responded Tashika Bronson in a quizzical voice. "That sermon was not just for listeners. There was so much seeing and doing as well: the newsprint, the church roof, the cartons, the residents joining in, the procession up and down the ramps. The action was as important as the words.

"Preachers overuse the vocabulary of speaking and listening, of calling and hearing.[10] If that is the only way we think about preaching, where does that leave people who cannot hear? What does it mean for people in the pew whose hearing is fine but who are more engaged through their eyes than their ears? How do we make the gospel accessible to them?

"My baby brother, Darryl, has been deaf since birth. As a little girl, I worried that he could not be saved because he would not hear the word of God. When I went to church with my parents, I used to pay extra attention to the sermon, even when I was bored, hoping that my hard work to hear the word of God would count for Darryl as well.

"Several years ago, when I was an M.Div. student, I got into a violent argument with a history professor who taught reformation studies. I objected to the obsessive emphasis on hearing the word of God.

"The professor quotes back at me Romans 10:17 that 'faith comes by hearing,' and then he adds what Martin Luther says—that God does not require of us 'the feet or the hands or any other member' but that God 'requires only the ears.'[11]

"I tell the professor he is reducing salvation to an auditory act, as though the Spirit can work only through the eardrum. His position leaves no room in the world for non-hearing people. It treats them as aliens. It labels them as stupid. I quote those painful lines from 'O For a Thousand Tongues to Sing': 'Hear him, ye deaf; his praise, ye dumb.' Then I ask, 'What about seeing the truth instead of hearing it?'[12]

"Then he starts quoting Calvin, on the dangers of images and how the ear is the gate to heaven. I say to him, 'So heaven has no entrance for my deaf brother!' "

As Tashika Bronson spoke, the class could feel her fury returning. She had the sound of a big sister defending her little brother from a bully. To Peter Linden it sounded like the holy anger of a prophet. God was raging against any understanding of preaching that would lock someone out of the gospel.

Then Tashika's tone suddenly softened. She explained that the reformation professor had not known about her deaf brother, and as soon as the words were out of her mouth, his face had fallen and he stopped throwing theology at her.

She stayed after class, and they talked. He apologized. He had not meant to hurt her. She accepted his apology and then said, "You were fighting as hard as I was. I was defending my brother. What were you defending?"

The professor thought a long time, and then he explained that he had grown weary in recent years of all the demands of what he called "special interest" groups. He felt battered by demands from ethnic groups, demands from the Third World, demands from feminists, and now yet another demand that challenged the tradition he stood for.

When the man was first ordained, the Christian faith seemed to him a vast continent. But starting back in the 1960s it appeared that one tidal wave after another was crumbling the shore line, and the continent was shrinking to an island, and soon even that would wash away.

Tashika said that she could still hear the mixture of sadness and fear in the professor's voice. She said that she often picked up the same tone among many pastors. They were weary of having to listen to so many different voices, to learn so many new ways to see the world, so many new ways to speak.

Tashika had responded to the professor, saying: "What you see as a shrinking island I see as a growing banquet table. More sections of the table are being set up all the time. News is spreading through the streets that everyone is invited as a guest of equal distinction—every ethnic group, girls, boys, women, men, deaf, poor, maimed, blind, lame. All of them. They are not special interest groups. They are people God has asked to come, and they refuse to be turned away at the door by those who are less hospitable than the host."

Tashika became less animated, and she acknowledged in a sober voice that she had sometimes been as angry as the professor had been. Sometimes, growing up, she had resented all the adjustments their family had to make to accommodate her deaf brother. She had looked with envy at families where everyone was born with all their senses intact.

"But one day," Tashika recalled, "I was signing with Darryl. I was getting to the point of fluency when I was not having to stop and think about the gestures. I was not pausing to translate things into audible language in the silence of my mind. The communication was flowing between us, and my brother's face was shining as I had never seen it shine before."

Tashika said that the point of her story was not that everyone must learn to sign. Instead, she offered the story as an invitation to preachers to present the fullness of God's communication with us. Again Tashika became very animated and spoke as if she had been taken over by a truth she could not suppress. "God does so much more than speak to us. God shapes us as a potter shapes clay. God blows on us as wind. God attracts us as light. God warms us as fire. God cools our thirst as water. God feeds us as bread and wine. God shows us in Christ that God's word is more than speech: 'The word became flesh and dwelt among us full of grace and truth.' "

Tashika fell silent, and then said: "I guess the sermon I most remember is the one I have always been waiting to hear. In some ways I am like Marjorie, preaching to counter the preaching that has done harm in the past.

"I often think of the confrontation between me and the reformation professor. It was typical of many heated conversations I had as a black woman in seminary. That professor assumed his position was normative while he disparaged the others as special interests. But it turned out that his interest was as special as anyone else's; he wanted to protect his shrinking continent, his shrinking island. I am suspicious of preachers who do not acknowledge the needs that feed their theology. Every preacher is a prism. Every preacher bends the light of God."

"But our job is to bend it as little as we can," said Eddie Hanson. The whole class appeared surprised to hear Eddie speak, including Eddie himself. He was the only one who had not participated in the vigorous discussion they had on authority.

Peter could still picture Eddie, his large muscular frame drawn all the way back into his chair while he followed the course of the discussion with the slightest movement of his eyes. He gave the impression of someone on a distant hill observing a battle he did not want to get caught in.

What Peter remembered most about Eddie Hanson was a conversation between the two of them after the third week of classes. Peter had asked him to come by the office to see if there were some way Eddie might become a more active participant in the seminar. Eddie was reluctant to make the appointment, but he did, and he came on time.

At first the conversation was awkward, the professor expressing concern about the student's quietness in class. But when Peter said, "I mention this only because I want you to get as much out of the course as possible and because I believe everyone has something to offer." Eddie sat up and responded, "But I don't believe the class is ready to hear what I have to say. None of the other students and teachers in this place has ever shown any interest when I have spoken."

Eddie's voice was a mixture of sadness and disdain, as if he were grieved that he had not been heard in the past and, to protect himself from further pain, had assumed a posture of superiority.

"What did you say that no one listened to?" Peter asked.

"I told them about my theology, which is very different from all of theirs. I mean more different than Katherine's is from Jason's, more different than Marjorie's is from Isaiah's."

Then Eddie told of his upbringing, how his father had played the drums and his mother had sung in the choir of the Holy Ghost Tabernacle of Prayer, a congregation Eddie described as a "pentecostal, holiness church."

Eddie explained that the sermon he most remembered was not the one he had told about in class, but rather a sermon delivered by a recruitment officer for a small religious college. The Holy

Ghost Tabernacle of Prayer was a regular contributor to the school through its mission offerings.

Eddie was a junior in high school when he heard the sermon. He had an above average academic record and had made the all-city football team as a right tackle. Several liberal arts colleges were interested in giving him an athletic scholarship because he had ability on the field and in the classroom, the kind of balanced student their catalogs said they sought.

Eddie would need all the financial support he could get. His father worked on an assembly line in a defense plant, which meant his employment depended on the flow of government contracts. There were many times when the family income was reduced to what Eddie's mother brought home from filling out slips in a dry cleaning establishment. They lived pay check to pay check, and they gave a tenth of that to their church before they spent their money for other things.

But any relief they felt at the possibility of a scholarship for Eddie was offset by their fear that a liberal institution of learning would rob their son of his faith and corrupt his holiness with the drugs and sex that the media had convinced them were rampant on every campus.

Because of the close religious bond he shared with his parents, Eddie agreed with their judgment and discouraged all recruiters until that Sunday when the preacher from the small religious college delivered a sermon on 1 Peter 2:9: "But ye are a chosen generation, a royal priesthood, a holy nation, a peculiar people; that ye should show forth the praises of him who hath called you out of darkness into his marvelous light."

The preacher used the verse in a way that confirmed the Hansons' worst fears about the colleges that had been badgering Eddie to accept their scholarship offers. It was all an effort to tempt their son away from God to the world. By way of contrast, the preacher described his campus, where "a life of holiness is our guiding ideal," where young people could hear the Holy Spirit telling them, "Ye are a chosen generation, a royal priesthood, a holy nation, a peculiar people." Young people who heard that calling in their hearts and had it confirmed by the anointing of the Holy Spirit and reinforced by a community of Christian care were not going to waste their gifts on drugs and other immoralities.

The sense of relief in Eddie's mother was so great that during the testimonials following the sermon she gave a witness to how the Holy Spirit had brought the preacher to speak directly to her family. Through his sermon she felt the Holy Spirit lifting and carrying away the burden on her heart.

As Eddie recounted all of this, he could see from Peter Linden's attentive face that the professor did not consider his story bizarre, and in turn Eddie's voice lost its mixture of sadness and disdain and became more confident in tone as he continued.

"So I went off to that college. There was no football team, but I got a scholarship anyway, since I signed up to be a ministerial major."

While he was there, Eddie fell under the spell of the professor of biblical languages, who was known for being the most Spirit-filled preacher in chapel and the most demanding teacher in the classroom. The professor had attended the same college as an undergraduate, but then he had gone off to a well-known mainline seminary, followed by an Ivy League graduate school to specialize in ancient Near Eastern studies. The man's learning was astounding to Eddie, especially the way he could draw upon his technical knowledge of the Bible to interpret Eddie's pentecostal holiness tradition.

"I'm here now in this seminary," explained Eddie, "because I hope some day to hold a position like his. I plan to go from here to graduate school."

Eddie told how he worked to get all A's in the language and exegetical courses, but that in the other courses he saw himself "just passing through." He signed up for "Preachers in Search of Their Voices" only because he needed one more course in pastoral studies for graduation, and this one fit conveniently between advanced Hebrew exegesis and the Romans translation seminar.

"I talk in those courses," said Eddie. "It's safe. Either you know how to parse the verb or you don't. I tried talking in theology and the introductory preaching class, but all we did was argue without getting anywhere. And I can see that the same thing would happen again between me and this class. What I hear when they speak is just a pack of people trying to fit God to their own experience. But the Holy Spirit blows where he wills.

"They talk of liberation, but all I hear are human programs for their own ideas. If you try to bring a revolution without changing

61

sinful human nature, you will only create more victims. I am not against the women preaching—we had them in our churches long before there was women's liberation—and I am certainly not against blacks finding justice. All the prophets of the Bible stand on their side. I believe in those things, but I believe in them because they have the anointing of the Spirit; they are of God.

"Everybody around here talks about 'being open' and 'being inclusive,' but I have not seen this place open to the Holy Spirit or open to speaking in tongues or open to the pentecostal holiness tradition. I am not worried about finding my voice. I want God's voice to sound in me by the power of the Spirit, by bringing the blessing of holiness to my heart and the unction of holiness to my lips and the power of holiness to my walk."

Ten years after their conversation, Peter could still remember the earnest piety in Eddie Hanson's voice. Whenever they met in the hall or happened to sit at the table in the cafeteria, Eddie was cordial, as though their conversation in Peter's office had at least established that Peter did not disparage Eddie's experience as a member of a pentecostal holiness church.

But in class Eddie always kept up his guard. Various students tried to draw Eddie into conversation during the beginning of the term. He responded politely but skirted any real theological engagement. After a few weeks, people just accepted him as the quiet member of the class.

Neither did Eddie reveal his pentecostal holiness perspective from the pulpit, except at the end of the term, when it was too late to influence their discussions.

Eddie Hanson's silence became for Peter Linden a reminder of the limitations not only of his own style of teaching, but also of the limitations of the entire seminary ethos. "Globalization" and "cross-cultural understanding" were the buzzwords of the day. Many students had taken trips to various countries around the globe as part of their theological education and had talked about the importance of reaching out to communicate across barriers. But here was someone representing another culture right in their midst, a devout member of the pentecostal holiness tradition, and they had cut him off when he spoke. Peter knew from some comments by colleagues that Eddie had not exaggerated the negative response he received to his earlier attempts to talk in theology and introductory preaching.

Peter Linden wondered: "Whose definition of diversity is the accepted one?"[13] The goals of openness and inclusivity that were touted by most of the students and faculty had become a barrier to hearing a tradition whose experience and theology were intractably different, a tradition that set itself apart from the dominant culture in order to be faithful to its experience and understanding of the Holy Spirit.

There was something of that same feeling of being set apart in the way Chung Won Kim described the Korean immigrant church he served. Like Eddie, he was very reserved in class. His silence, however, was of an entirely different kind. It was the silence of someone who was preparing to speak by gathering together all the words that others had put in the air.

"I observe much suffering," was the first thing that Chung Won Kim said to the class. "Katherine has suffered from a church that acted like a family of men ignoring women. Jason has suffered the loss of a friend to a land mine. Dorian has suffered the loss of his ancestors to the plow. Roger tells of suffering families in happy-looking houses. Marjorie has suffered with an abused woman. Isaiah has suffered the loss of his father to war. Karen has seen suffering at the center where she works. Tashika has told of the suffering of her deaf brother. Much suffering meets at this table of preachers."

Chung Won Kim had gray eyes and salt-and-pepper hair. His speech carried a melody of oriental pitches that caused the others to hear their own tongue in a new key.

"As you spoke, I recalled my childhood in Korea. Especially during Jason's story of the land mine, I remembered my family's escaping south from North Korea as the war started. I was five. We were hiding beneath a willow tree at night when the border patrol got suspicious and sprayed the air with bullets. Some leaves and branches showered down on us. Then the patrol walked on, and we escaped. But many friends and relatives never made it across the line."

Chung Won Kim told what it was like after a bomb raid or a howitzer attack. The survivors would stumble out on the cratered streets filled with rubble and lined with charred ruins. All they could do at first was look at each other. Their amazement at still being alive was too great for words.

Then Chung Won said, "Anyone who makes it to the twenty-first century is a survivor from great horror. The job of preachers is to make sure that the survivors never forget what happened to the others."

Rummaging in his canvas book bag, Chung Won explained: "Since others have quoted from books, let me read a passage. It helps me say what I heard you saying." Chung Won Kim pulled out a copy of *Faith in History and Society*, by Johann Baptist Metz, and began an expository sermon, using the theologian's words as his text and the class memories as illustrations. He read:

> There are some very different kinds of memories. There are those in which we just do not take the past seriously enough: memories in which the past becomes a paradise without danger, a refuge from our present disappointments—the memory of the "good old days."[14]

"That sounds like the newcomers to Clydes Corners," said Chung Won Kim. "They are looking for the ideal country church and are building beautiful homes, but they do not understand the farmers whose tractors are rusting in the front yards.

" 'The memory of the good old days' also seems to have influenced the people who decorated this room with the old clock and the pictures of Victorian gentlemen. I do not mean by this to sound too critical. In my own church we have difficulties because there are three different generations with different memories that result in different values and hopes. My generation, the war generation, represents the first wave of immigrants to our church. Sometimes I slip into preaching as though all of my listeners were shaped by the same experience as myself.

"I must always be remembering that there are others—what we call the 'second generation,' the most recent immigrants who are facing all the acute problems of being strangers in a foreign land. And then there is the so-called transgeneration, the generation in between the first and second, the ones who were born in Korea and were educated as children in America and are comfortable with the English language.

"Each group has a different idea of what the church should be, and this makes it very difficult to find my voice as a preacher in a way that can hold us together and yet give us direction for the future.[15] But I have figured out this much: While I work to become open to the generations that are following my own, I must not let any of us forget what did happen in the past."

Then Chung Won Kim read some more from Johann Baptist Metz: "War as an inferno is obliterated from ['the good old days'] . . . what seems to remain is only the adventure experienced long ago."

Chung Won put down the book and looked up to say: "Dorian's ancestors were plowed over. Jason's friend, killed. Isaiah's father, killed. My relatives, killed. All of them were killed in the inferno of war. We have remembered them here, but the world forgets. Metz says:

> The past is filtered through a harmless cliche: everything dangerous, oppressive and demanding has vanished from it: it seems deprived of all future. In this way, memory can easily become a "false consciousness" of our past and an opiate for our present.

"The players in *That Championship Season* use the past as an opiate, celebrating the game they cheated to win. The Clyde family uses the past as an opiate, hanging on to the couch while forgetting about the Indian mounds. Tashika's professor in reformation studies uses the past as an opiate—remembering when theology seemed like a whole continent instead of an island in a violent sea."

Once again Chung Won Kim started to read from Metz: " 'But there is another form of memory: there are dangerous memories, memories which make demands on us.'

"Marjorie's memory of the abused woman is a dangerous memory; it demands a new way to preach. Dorian's memory of tribal customs suppressed by the missionaries is a dangerous memory; it demands reclaiming what has been lost, redefining what it means to be Christian. Katherine's memory of feeling like an ignored woman in a family of men is a dangerous memory; it demands the therapy of the religious imagination. Karen's memory of the junior high service at the center is a dangerous memory; it demands giving access to everyone, every group.

"Metz says, 'Every rebellion against suffering is fed by the subversive power of remembered suffering.' That is the task of proclaiming the gospel into the twenty-first century: to lead the rebellion against suffering by remembering the suffering of the past. Our voices as preachers will be most effective when we sound like thankful subversives."

"Thankful subversives?" asked one of the students.

Chung Won Kim looked up with a puzzled expression on his own face. Then he said: "Oh, that's right. I forgot to tell my most memorable sermon. That's where *thankful* comes from.

"We were in a Red Cross tent. We were having a service with the Lord's Supper. The preacher starts the words of institution: 'The Lord Jesus on the night when he was betrayed took bread, and when he had given thanks. . . . ' The preacher stops right there. Then he asks: 'What are betrayal and thanksgiving doing next to each other? Why are they in the same sentence?' He reminds us that the betrayal of Christ brought crucifixion at the hands of soldiers. Then he recalls our suffering at the hands of soldiers. He says every time we gather at Christ's table we remember betrayal, we remember suffering, we 'proclaim the Lord's death until he comes.'

"But the memory of betrayal must not choke out thanksgiving. If it does, then only bitterness follows. Instead, we are to follow Jesus. He knew betrayal. He knew suffering. He did not deny suffering. But on the night he was betrayed, he gave thanks."

When Chung Won Kim finished, the seminar table seemed more like an altar than a piece of classroom furniture. Peter Linden observed that the note pads and books that covered the table appeared to him like the leftovers of a meal they had all shared together. And Karen Steel remarked as they stood to leave the table: "Yes, a meal, with everyone bringing something, and everyone at least tasting what the others offer. That's how we will find our voices for proclaiming the gospel into the twenty-first century."

Chapter 3

New Voices

Gathering Together All We Have Heard

Karen Steel compared "Preachers in Search of Their Voices" to a common meal, with everyone bringing something to pass around. But like most potluck suppers, people took ample portions of their favorites and showed themselves reluctant to try what was strange and new. At least one person thought of leaving the meal altogether. Between the second and third meeting of the class, a student came by Peter Linden's office to consider dropping the course.

Jason Kirk, the pastor of the Clydes Corners church, let out a sigh as he sat down in the flowered couch opposite Peter's chair with the cracked green leather seat: "I'm troubled by some of the things I've heard in class. I hope you won't jump on me for saying this. I don't mean to be closed minded, but I was disturbed by the anger of some of the women.

"When Marjorie Hudson spoke about the sermon for the battered woman, and when Tashika Bronson talked about her deaf brother, I felt—well, I felt judged. I've preached that sermon on reconciliation that Marjorie's pastor preached. I've preached it again and again in my ministry. And I've preached how God calls to us and how deaf we are to his Word. God does want us reconciled; God does speak to us, doesn't he?"

"Yes, Jason, of course, God does. I didn't hear Marjorie or Tashika denying either of those things. But it's clear that you heard something in their anger that frightened you."

"I was afraid because what they said sounded like an attack on my forty-two years of ministry. When you've got a church fighting over something like that red horsehair couch, you don't have much energy left for someone to question the character of your preaching.

"I sympathized with Tashika's history professor, the one who said he felt like the continent of theology had shrunk down to an island, and now the island is about to be washed away by tidal waves. I felt the pounding of the waves in the women's anger. Why are they so personally angry?"

"Because, Jason, their ministry means as much to them as yours does to you. And besides, it involves a lot more than personal anger. I'm reading that book Tashika told us about, *This Bridge Called My Back: Writings by Radical Women of Color*. The women tell how they often feel they're 'dumping' their words 'into a very deep and very dark hole.'[1] They're angry because they've been ignored.

"Marjorie and Tashika speak as members of an 'outgroup,' those who are pushed to the side by the dominant society.[2] Tashika's circle, with everyone taking turns at the center, finally gives the outgroups a chance to be heard: the women, the persons of color, the deaf, the abused.

"Imagine that all of your life you were forced to stand on the rim of the circle or even outside it. When you finally got to the center for the first time, you looked out and saw an abused woman whose wounds you had dressed or you saw your deaf brother. Would you not be angry, not just angry personally, but angry that these people were considered peripheral?"

While Jason Kirk and he looked at one another in silence, Peter Linden felt the Spirit vexing his own heart with difficult questions: How would he and Jason respond to the anger of the women? Would they disparage the women as representing special interests? Would they grow frustrated at the interruption of their agendas and lash back in anger?

Peter figured that Jason Kirk was less apt to succumb to these destructive impulses than other men. At least Jason recognized what was happening to himself. Emotional honesty alone was not an adequate response, but it was a first step.

"I see what you're getting at about the outgroup," said Jason, "but I'm still not sure that I have the energy to stay in the course."

"Well, everyone deserves a rest in life, and you, Jason, have worked long and hard as a pastor. Still I have a hunch you may find yourself more exhausted if you drop out than if you stay with it. When you came out of the war, you had no peace until you found a theology that made sense. Now the approaches that once satisfied you are breaking down, and your old disquiet is returning.

"I have no replacement for the old answers. All I know is that we need each other, Jason. The class needs to hear about the red horsehair couch. We need to remember the gritty work of being a pastor in a place like Clydes Corners. To lose you would be a diminishment of the fullness of the church, just as it would be a diminishment if we lost Marjorie or Tashika or anyone else. Gathered around that seminar table, we're learning that faith ranges far beyond what any of us had ever imagined. Maybe that's what Christ meant about people coming from north and south and east and west to sit at table in the reign of God. Those aren't just directions on the globe, they're locations in the heart."

"I guess I had hoped things would be simpler," said Jason.

"Yes, I suppose all of us wish things were simpler. But from all of your years as a pastor, you know they seldom ever are."

Jason nodded in agreement and stood up from the flowered couch in Peter's office. His face revealed that he was still mulling things over. They shook hands, and Peter showed Jason to the door.

As Jason's footfalls echoed down the seminary corridor, Peter heard him faintly whistling "Spirit of the Living God, Fall Afresh on Me." Peter imagined all the members of the class joining in and singing the hymn together, a prayer for the work that lay ahead of them:

> Spirit of the living God, fall afresh on me!
> Spirit of the living God, fall afresh on me.
> Melt me! Mold me! Fill me! Use me.
> Spirit of the living God, fall afresh on me.[3]

The music faded from Peter's mind, and he thought of the hunger of the human heart, the hunger to taste the Spirit, the hunger to be remolded and filled with the presence of the living God. Peter thought of all the hundreds of times that he and preachers like Jason had led their congregations in hymns and prayers, asking God to refashion who they were. Peter stopped and wondered: Perhaps we have sought the gift of renewal without considering what it really means. Perhaps we have become too chummy with God, assuming God would refrain from any judgment or anger, like the judgment and anger of the outgroups, of Marjorie and Tashika.

Peter thought of the eighteenth-century Hasids who knew the risk of prayer. When Rabbi Uri of Strelisk left his house each morning to pray, he always told the family how to dispose of his belongings in case his praying should kill him. Asked by a friend why he did this, the rabbi explained that he began his prayers by invoking God's name and then offering a petition for mercy. "Who knows," said the rabbi, "what the Lord's power will do to me in that moment after I have invoked [the Holy Name] and before I beg for mercy?"[4]

Peter sat in his office, thinking of the rabbi's response and repeating in his mind the words of the hymn. Suddenly he realized that the awesome God, the God whose name is never to be lightly invoked, was answering the prayer that Jason had whistled down the corridor: "Melt me, mold me, fill me, use me." God was answering the prayer through the anger of Marjorie and Tashika. God was answering the prayer through the anger of the outgroups.

"Melt me. Mold me."

Peter recalled watching glass blowers at work. He remembered the white hot furnace and the glowing mass of viscous material at the end of the blower's tube. Sometimes because of chemical impurity or the wrong molecular structure, the glass could not endure the process.

"Melt me, mold me." Did Jason Kirk, did Peter Linden, did all the class members have the resilience of soul to let God melt them and mold them through the witness of the women, people with physical disabilities, the abused, the ignored?

"Spirit of the living God, fall afresh on me," prayed Peter Linden. Then, like Rabbi Uri of Strelisk, he stopped and wondered what God's power would do to him, Peter Linden, a preacher of the word of God.

Peter became aware of the gift of his heart beating, the gift of his lungs breathing. With renewed energy he prayed again: "Spirit of the living God, fall afresh on me."

Once more Peter stopped. A vision of a glass blower pumping the furnace bellows filled Peter's mind, and he started offering the rest of the prayer, stopping after each petition, wondering in silence if he would live to make it to the next request:

> Melt me.
> Mold me.
> Fill me.
> Use me.
> Spirit of the living God, fall afresh on me.

Whether it was the conversation in Peter Linden's office or some secret motion of the Spirit in the soul, Jason Kirk stayed on in the course. Near the end of the semester, he delivered a sermon that showed that God had melted and molded him through the preaching of his colleagues.

And Jason was not the only one who changed. Many others did as well. Whenever Peter Linden tried to understand these changes, he thought of a sermon by Katherine Carr. Her sermon kept returning in class discussions because it so directly addressed the theme of the course.

The title of Katherine's sermon came from a youngster who had asked a spontaneous question during a church service she had led. The child was standing on the chancel steps with other boys and girls who had come forward for the children's sermon. Before Katherine had spoken her first words to them, the boy asked, "What does the voice of God sound like?"

He spoke loudly enough for the question to echo through the entire sanctuary. It was the kind of behavior from a child that usually made the congregation laugh. But not this Sunday. The earnestness of the child was so apparent in his face and voice that the congregation grew very still.

Katherine often did not like children's sermons because they seemed contrived—an adult's version of how children ought to think about God. But here was a child asking in his own way a theological question that meant as much to him as any question the adults might raise. "What does the voice of God sound like?"

Looking at the attentive faces of the congregation, Katherine realized that the little boy's question had preempted the children's sermon she had prepared. They were all waiting to see

71

how their pastor would answer the question, "What does the voice of God sound like?"

Katherine thought of the new life that was growing within her. In recent weeks she had often been snapped awake in the middle of the night by the sharp kicks of the child she would soon deliver. She imagined how she would answer if it were her little one asking, "What does the voice of God sound like?" Surely she would not say, "The voice of God is just a metaphor, a way of speaking about something mysterious." That was an adult's explanation. And the child had been clear in his emphasis, he wanted to know about the *voice* of God.

Suddenly Katherine realized that she was daydreaming and that the congregation and the children were waiting for her reply. She began slowly, saying: "The voice of God sounds like. . . . " Katherine drew the words out as long as she could while she prayed desperately that God would speak and give her an answer.

She started once again: "The voice of God sounds like . . . like your best friend, like someone you trust, someone you can really talk things over with. The voice of God sounds like your mother or your father or your favorite baby sitter when they comfort you because you're having a bad dream in the night. You hear them next to your bed, calling: 'Everything's all right. Everything's all right. I'm right here beside you.' "

The example of a voice in the darkness made Katherine think of the call of Samuel. So she continued her sermon by telling how Samuel heard God calling three times in the night. Each time Samuel ran to Eli, thinking his friend had called him. Finally, Eli realized what was happening and told Samuel it was God.

"So sometimes," explained Katherine, "it's not easy to recognize the voice of God on our own. We often need our friends to help us."

That Sunday afternoon after church, Katherine kept returning to the child's question, considering it from different angles.

"What does the voice of God sound like?"

Katherine gradually realized that her response was more than a way of answering the little boy. It was the birth of an insight that had been developing week by week in class: Preachers need one another to hear God calling in ways they cannot identify on their own. Preachers need to serve each other as Eli served Samuel, not just at the start of their ministries, but as the years pass by and God speaks in new and unexpected ways.

"What does the *voice* of God sound like?"

The way the child had emphasized the word *voice* made Katherine think of the term *voice*, which she had studied in her doctoral program in English and which Peter Linden had adapted to the title of the course. The study of modern literature had impressed upon Katherine the importance of the writer's individual voice.[5] So when she began to study theology, she was struck by the impact of the community on the voice of each biblical writer.

"The community," explained Katherine, "has continued through the centuries to shape the voice of its preachers. But nowadays the community is filled with a diversity of voices. Look at this class. Think about the global village. What is the impact of all these different voices on the voice of the preacher today?

"I think the title of this course is accurate, 'Preachers in Search of Their Voices' that's who we are; that's what we're doing. We are aware that the preaching voice we have used in the past is not adequate in the present. So we have become preachers in search of our voices, in search of the most effective way to proclaim the gospel into the twenty-first century.

"When we listen to one another, we begin to hear the diversity of voices that fills the community of God. Our diversity represents a more complete answer to the little boy who asked, 'What does the voice of God sound like?'

"I pray that child will grow up to see not only the truth of my answer but also its inadequacy. I told him, 'The voice of God sounds like your best friend.' Yes, the voice of God does sound like our best friend. But the voice of God also sounds like the stranger, the alien, the one who cries out in hurt and hunger.

"We are preachers in search of our voices because we want the voice of God to be as richly present in our preaching as it possibly can be."

Nearly everyone in class liked the opening to Katherine's sermon, the telling of the story of the little boy, and her answer to him. But they were divided about the idea of being in search of their voices.

Chung Won Kim explained how important the transcendence

of God was in his theology, a theme that often sounded in his sermons. He feared that the idea of preachers' searching for their voices would dilute the power of God's word. "It was by the transcendent power of the word," Chung Won Kim said, "that my family survived the war and came to terms with our grief over all who died. The Bible says, 'Thus saith the Lord,' not 'thus have the preachers found their voices.' "

All the while that Chung Won Kim spoke, Jason Kirk nodded his head in agreement. And it was one of the rare times when Eddie Hanson felt there might be at least some support in the class for the theology of his holiness tradition. He joined in the conversation, expanding on Chung Won's statement and affirming, "The Holy Spirit is not ours to control. We do not search for the Spirit. The Holy Spirit comes and finds us and anoints us with power and blessing and the calling to preach."

Katherine Carr answered back, taking on both Chung Won and Eddie Hanson at the same time: "It's a false dichotomy to contrast God's word and our search, the coming of the Holy Spirit and our seeking for the Spirit's presence. When I took the prophets course, I learned that many of their oracles are carefully crafted literary forms. The words 'Thus saith the Lord' arose from a search for the prophet's voice. They often reworked their material, sometimes in the light of cultic norms, sometimes independent of the prophetic guilds.[6] That doesn't make what they preached any less the word of God. Instead, it heightens my wonder at the way God works through human efforts. Searching for our voice as preachers is our way of honoring the word of God with integrity, it is our way of opening ourselves to the Spirit."

Tashika Bronson, Dorian White Elk, and Roger Hawkins all agreed that Katherine's sermon clarified their struggles in the pulpit.

Tashika explained that she had grown up hearing only men preach, and although she had fond memories of her childhood pastors, she felt a need to develop a different "voice," faithful to her tradition but reflective of who she was as a woman.

Dorian White Elk said that he was looking for a voice that would blend Indian culture and biblical faith.

Roger Hawkins said that he was searching for a voice that would make a clearer distinction between suburban culture and the gospel of Jesus Christ.

As a result of Katherine's sermon and the discussion that followed, the concept of "voice" became more helpful than when Peter had first introduced the word. The preachers found it gave them a term for describing not simply their individual sermons, but the cumulative impact of their efforts. The "voice" of the preacher became a way for each of them to ask: What do I sound like to those who hear me week after week? What "voice" emerges through my preaching over time?

The term *voice* suggested that the renewal of preaching into the twenty-first century involved more than mastering this or that homiletical method. It called for expanding and deepening the sources that fed the mind and heart of the preacher.

The improvement of any one sermon might rest on finding a helpful commentary or reworking the outline. But the improvement of a preacher's "voice" required an ongoing discipline of prayer and theological reflection.

While Peter sat in his office chair and perused the names of the preachers on the class list, he conjured up the sound and sight of each student. And as he listened and watched them through the distance of time, he remembered how their "voices" as preachers were so much more than the content of their sermons. Even when he forgot the details of what they said, he could picture where they focused their eyes, how they stood and shifted on their feet, how they held onto the pulpit rail or used their hands in flowing gestures. He could hear again their speech and its variations of pitch and loudness and pace. It was no wonder to Peter why his heart beat a little faster whenever a preacher stepped into the pulpit, for he was always eager to know: How will the streams of God flow through this person to the congregation?

Peter pictured Marjorie Hudson standing before the class in the seminary chapel. Marjorie carried into the pulpit the same commanding presence that was hers in the emergency room and around the seminar table. The members of "Preachers in Search of Their Voices" never forgot Marjorie's story of the abused woman. The class discussion of sermons often considered: How would this sound to a battered woman?

Now that Marjorie had a place in the pulpit, she delivered the sermons she had never heard as a disgruntled listener. However, her anger about the distortions of past preaching was tempered by her compassion as a nurse. She knew how difficult it can be to make a diagnosis and to prescribe the right treatment in medicine, and she was certain the same was true of being a physician to the soul. As a result, she balanced her dissatisfaction with the homiletical tradition with a sense of humor.

Anger and humor both were present in her sermon "The Forgotten Healer," based on Luke 10:25-37. Marjorie's opening sentence still rang in Peter's head:

"Oh no! not another sermon on the good Samaritan!"

Marjorie went on to tell that most of the sermons she had heard on the text seemed to have a standard outline that was passed from preacher to preacher. There was usually a joke about the priest who passed by on the other side because he was going to a church meeting, and a joke about the Levite who passed by because he was going to the same meeting and was later than the priest.

As a nurse, Marjorie resented these jokes. They made her think of times when her unit at the hospital was understaffed. She often ignored one patient in order to tend to another.

When Marjorie came to seminary it was a relief for her to learn that the priest and the Levite might have passed by because under ritual law they would have been counted unclean if they touched a dead man, and they might have taken the victim for dead if he were not moving. She reflected: "Perhaps they were rushing to help someone else who was desperate. If they touched a dead man it would defile them. Then they would be a help to no one."

Marjorie acknowledged that she was speculating. "Whether I'm right or wrong about it," she said, "I don't intend to put others down in order to lift someone else up. Honoring the compassion of the Samaritan does not require attacking the priest and the Levite."

Marjorie wondered how many pastors had fallen prey to the accusation their priest and Levite jokes encouraged. How often had someone unfairly charged the pastors with being "unfeeling," when there were simply more people who needed them than they could tend at one time?

Marjorie said she wanted to focus on the most neglected figure in the parable. As she moved one page of her pulpit notes to the side, Peter assumed that Marjorie would talk about the victim. Instead, she read aloud from the biblical text:

> The next day [the Samaritan] took out two denarii, gave them to
> the innkeeper, and said, "Take care of him; and when I come back,
> I will repay you whatever more you spend."

"Have you ever considered the role of the innkeeper in this
parable?" asked Marjorie. She pointed out that the victim of the
mugging would probably need several weeks to recover; the text
had described him as half dead.

Marjorie spoke with the full force of her twenty-five years of
nursing: "It's one thing to deliver emergency care, but it's
another to provide long-term care—the tedium of lifting a spoon
to someone else's lips, the drudgery of emptying the bed pan, the
burden of turning the body and changing the dressings, the
exhaustion of waking in the night to the moaning of the victim
who relives the violence in a nightmare.

"And the innkeeper," said Marjorie, "was to do all of this,
trusting that the Samaritan would someday return and cover the
full bill. It would be hard enough to trust someone who came
from the more respected ranks of society, but this was a
Samaritan, an outcast, a member of a suspect minority. The
Samaritan was obviously a good and decent human being.
Nevertheless, the innkeeper would have to overcome all of the
prejudices that were part of the culture in order to take the
Samaritan at his word. Under the circumstances, the innkeeper
had to be a good neighbor to the Samaritan as well as to the
victim."

Then Marjorie explained that the Mishna tells of some Levites
who traveled the same road eastward from Jerusalem and who
left a sick companion in the care of a woman innkeeper. Some
scholars suggest this might be the same inn as in the parable.[7]

"The forgotten healer," said Marjorie, "is the woman
innkeeper. The forgotten healer is all the women who through
the centuries have been nursing the beds of their sick children,
their elderly parents, the soldiers burned and mutilated on the
front line. They have been feeding and bandaging and tending
the victims, and they have yet to be fully paid.

"I've often wondered whether the Samaritan kept his promise
to the innkeeper: 'When I come back, I will repay you whatever
more you spend.'[8] I have no doubt that the Samaritan made the
promise in good faith. But as a minority person, he was likely to

be the last hired and the first fired. Perhaps he would be unable to cover the bill in the future, not because he was dishonest, but because he did not have the money.

"That is the way it has been for the Samaritans and the innkeepers of this world. Those with the least resources have had to join together to bear the burden of tending to the most desperate.

"We do not know whether the Samaritan returned and the innkeeper's costs were paid in full. But we do know this: The forgotten healers are beginning to revise the story of the good Samaritan in order to encourage justice as well as compassion."

Then Katherine concluded with a parable she titled "Good Samaritan II," as if it were a sequel to the highly successful original.[9]

"Good Samaritan II" featured a congregation of compassionate Christians. One Sunday they discover on their steps a mugging victim who has staggered out of a nearby alley. They care for the victim and provide whatever is needed. A few weeks later in the same alley the same thing happens again. Once more the church responds with compassion. But upon its happening a third time, the people who have given long-term care to the earlier victims agitate to do something about the alley itself.

"I do not know," said Marjorie, "how the parable ends. I only know it is time for us to listen to the forgotten healers."

The class discussion that followed Marjorie's sermon started on a note of affirmation, but then became more acrimonious.

Marjorie's description of long-term care sounded a deep chord in Isaiah Thompson, who had attended his mother for several years after she had a series of debilitating strokes. Her small savings were quickly wiped out by her long-term illness, and he remembered his bitterness when he tried to get more house calls from the visiting nurse and ran into stone walls in the labyrinth of medical care.

But Isaiah was also disturbed by the sermon, in particular by Marjorie's introduction to her new parable. She had said in the pulpit: "The biblical story is no longer adequate; it needs to be extended and revised."

He felt Marjorie devalued the Bible. He feared that her creative approach would encumber the Bible with the imaginings

78

of preachers, which in turn would corrode the authority of Scripture.

Isaiah's reservation touched off a number of other responses in class. The debate revealed sharp differences about the use of the Bible. Jason Kirk, Karen Steel, and Chung Won Kim joined with Isaiah. They felt Marjorie speculated too freely about the Bible. She displaced the authority of the scriptural story with her experience as a nurse and the parable of her own creation, "Good Samaritan II."

But Katherine Carr, Tashika Bronson, and Dorian White Elk all appreciated Marjorie's approach. Drawing upon Katherine's earlier sermon, "What Does the Voice of God Sound Like?" Tashika Bronson said: "I believe that Marjorie was modeling a new kind of 'voice' in the pulpit, a voice guided by feminist principles. She paid attention to an ignored woman, and she wrote a new parable to bring the truth of God into our lives now."[10]

Peter agreed that Marjorie's sermon represented a new voice that was emerging through the impact of feminist interpretation. He had heard this voice gaining strength over the twenty years that he had been teaching homiletics.

Reaching into his book bag for Elisabeth Schüssler Fiorenza's *Bread Not Stone*, Peter turned to a passage that had helped him understand the nature of this new preaching voice. He told the class: "Schüssler Fiorenza makes a distinction between treating the Bible as an archetype or a prototype." Then he read to them:

An archetype is "usually construed as an ideal form that establishes an unchanging pattern." . . . However . . . a prototype is not a binding, timeless pattern, but one critically open to the possibility, even the necessity of its own transformation.[11]

"Marjorie used the Bible," explained Peter, "as a prototype, not an archetype. Her new parable, 'Good Samaritan II,' treats the Bible as 'critically open to the possibility, even the necessity of its own transformation.' Am I being fair to you, Marjorie?"

"Yes, that's the spirit of what I'm trying to do. I believe deeply in Jesus Christ, but I often feel choked by the Christian past. I think I'm a combination of Katherine's sermon and Schüssler

Fiorenza's distinction. I'm searching for a prototypical voice in the pulpit."

Marjorie's search was clearly not the same as Jason's or Isaiah's. The struggle for a distinctive voice took its own form in each preacher. But there was a common pattern to the diversity of their efforts. Despite their theological differences, all of them were influenced by personal memory, by the traditions that raised them, by liberation movements, by the societal suspicion of authority, by the impact of the media, and by a desire to make sense of a world in chaos.

Peter could feel the passion of these forces not only in their preaching but also in their praying and singing. There was a hymn that had become a favorite on the seminary campus during the 1980s. The way the students sang the hymn gave a clue to the formation of their voices as preachers. Lost in song, they broke beyond the self-consciousness of their homiletical efforts to the spiritual origins of their preaching, to the source of their most compelling voice in the pulpit. They sang:

> I, the Lord of sea and sky,
> I have heard my people cry.
> All who dwell in dark and sin
> my hand will save.
> I who made the stars of night,
> I will make their darkness bright.
> Who will bear my light to them?
> Whom shall I send?
> Is it I, Lord?
> I have heard you calling in the night.
> I will go, Lord, if you lead me.
> I will hold your people in my heart.[12]

"I have heard you calling in the night," sang Jason Kirk, whose sleep had been haunted by the nightmares of his friend blown to pieces by a land mine. Jason's voice in the pulpit still carried the grief of that calling in the night.

"I have heard you calling in the night," sang Marjorie Hudson, who had tended the battered woman in the emergency room. Marjorie's voice in the pulpit still carried the burden of that calling in the night.

"I have heard you calling in the night," sang Isaiah Thompson, whose mother had quoted scripture to comfort him in the dark when the electricity went off. Isaiah's voice in the pulpit still carried the assurance of that calling in the night.

"I have heard you calling in the night," sang Chung Won Kim, who had escaped the soldiers firing machine guns into the darkness. Chung Won's voice in the pulpit still carried the terror of that calling in the night.

"I have heard you calling in the night," sang Katherine Carr, who had thought of the call of Samuel when the little boy asked, "What does the voice of God sound like?" Katherine's voice in the pulpit still carried the wonder of that calling in the night.

Each had heard God calling in the night in a particular way, and their different calls had given rise to different voices in the pulpit.

"When you sing to God," said Peter, "I hear the depth of soul that feeds a preacher's voice. Bring to the pulpit the passion you bring to your song."

Then Peter quoted George Herbert's seventeenth-century admonition to preachers, about "dipping and seasoning all our words and sentences in our hearts before they come into our mouths . . . so that the auditors may plainly perceive that every word is heart-deep."[13]

"Let your voice in the pulpit be 'heart-deep,'" said Peter, "the passion of your preaching as heart-deep as your song. But do not stop at the boundary of your own heart. Dip and season your words in the experience of those who are unlike yourself. Justo and Catherine González remind us to preach nothing that we 'would not dare say before those other Christians who are not present.'[14]

"Preach the gospel with a voice that's heart-deep and world-wide."

Some of the preachers in the class said that Peter Linden's vision was too idealistic. The pressures of the parish would never allow them to develop a voice that was heart-deep and worldwide.

Jason Kirk said, "Come to Clydes Corners and tell the folks fighting over the red horsehair couch that their pastor needs a voice that is heart-deep and worldwide."

Before Peter could respond, the pastors reminded one another that they hungered for a vision to give direction to the weekly labor of their preaching. It was why they signed up for the course in the first place.

The group fell silent. While the antique clock sent its gentle pulse through the air, Peter thought of the nineteenth-century preachers whose pictures hung on the walls of the seminar room. They had all joined the great cloud of witnesses which is described in the book of Hebrews. Peter imagined them looking down on the scene and cheering the whole class on, because from their vantage point they had a vision that was heart-deep and worldwide. Peter could almost hear them chanting to the beat of the clock:

> Claim the vision now;
> claim the vision now.
> Heart-deep, world wide,
> heart-deep, world wide,
> heart-deep, world wide.

It may have been that the members of the class also heard the great cloud of witnesses in their hearts, because as the term went on their voices started to become heart-deep and worldwide.

There was, for example, the revelation that came to Roger Hawkins through the preaching of Isaiah Thompson.

Isaiah stood in the pulpit and, taking a small well-worn Bible out of the inside pocket of his suit coat, read selected verses from Psalm 78:

> Give ear, O my people, to my teaching;
>   incline your ears to the words of my mouth.
> I will open my mouth in a parable;
>   I will utter dark sayings from of old. . . .
> [God] divided the sea and let them pass through it,
>   and made the waters stand like a heap. . . .
> He split rocks open in the wilderness,
>   and gave them drink abundantly as from the deep. . . .
> Yet they sinned still more against him. . . .
> They spoke against God, saying,
>   "Can God spread a table in the wilderness? . . . "
> They did not keep in mind [God's] power,
>   or the day when [God] redeemed them from the foe.

When Isaiah finished his reading, he took time to tell what an honor he considered it to be to stand in the pulpit. He invited the congregation to join in prayer and beseeched the Spirit to lead them all to the throne of grace. Through these opening words of introduction and prayer, the class caught the essential character of Isaiah's voice as a preacher. It was self-evident from the dignity of his speech and bearing that Isaiah considered himself to be standing on holy ground.

Isaiah had invited a number of African American sisters and brothers, some from the seminary and others from his church, to be present. He explained to the class that the vocal support of the congregation was an integral part of his tradition.

As the sermon started and Peter Linden heard the congregation responding, he thought of the communal wisdom preserved in the oral traditions of African American preaching. Instead of leaving preachers all alone to wonder whether their words were being heard, the congregation joined in the sermon as a community event. When the preacher was connecting to their lives, they affirmed the sermon with "Amens!" When the preacher wandered ineffectually, they redirected the sermon with cries of "Come on now, preach it." They had such an active part in the preaching that the sermon was as much theirs as it was the preacher's.

Isaiah Thompson started his sermon in a voice that was nearly as soft as that of Dorian White Elk, but there was a bright overtone in Isaiah's voice that sounded like distant trumpets marching closer and closer as the sermon developed.

Isaiah painted a picture of the wilderness where the Hebrews wandered. He described the rock and the sand and the heat rising up in waves. The trumpet in his voice drew nearer as he announced: "There was no cloud, no tree, no shade, but only the sun, a ball of solid white fire in the middle of the sky burning and baking and scorching everything in sight. The Hebrews cried out: 'Can God spread a table in the wilderness?' "

Isaiah did not answer the question right away. Instead, he began to expand the dimensions of the wilderness to the neighborhood around his own parish, to the street people, to the drug addicts, to the food cupboard and the soup kitchen that his church and several others were running. He told of weeks when the shelves were down to the last few cans of beans and soup, and he and the other pastors would ask themselves: "Can God spread a table in the wilderness?"

Then Isaiah extended the wilderness into the stories he had heard in class: the wilderness of the deaf in the world of the hearing, the wilderness of the abused in the world of violence, the wilderness of spiritual starvation in the world of the suburbs.

The description of every barren place and every barren condition ended with the same question: "Can God spread a table in the wilderness?"

Soon the whole class was as desperate as those Hebrews wandering beneath the blazing sun. But just when the congregation felt ready to die in the wilderness, the sermon took a dramatic turn.

Isaiah's voice softened as he puzzled the truth out of the biblical text. His brothers and sisters immediately caught the shift in tone, and their responses lessened for a moment. Some one called out, "Fix it, Preacher, fix it."

This request to "fix it" struck Peter Linden as something that all preachers, no matter what their tradition, needed to remember. Peter thought of the many dreary sermons he had heard, where the preacher described the brokenness of the world but gave no hint at all of how God could empower people to "fix it."

"Even when the congregation does not speak aloud," Peter thought, "the preacher needs to hear the cry of the heart: 'Fix it, Preacher, fix it.' "

Isaiah Thompson picked up his Bible and dug deeper into the text to learn how to "fix it." He read: "They did not keep in mind God's power, or the day when he redeemed them from the foe." Then in a stronger voice, like someone who is delighted to find the missing piece of a puzzle, Isaiah repeated to himself and to the congregation: "They did not keep in mind God's power.

"When Pharaoh and his commanders ordered their chariots to thunder upon the path dividing the Red Sea, they did not keep in mind the power of God.

"When Nebuchadnezzar and his attendants fired up the furnace to destroy the servants of the Lord, they did not keep in mind the power of God.

"When the disciples fled from the garden and hid in fear, they did not keep in mind the power of God.

"When the soldiers beat and mocked and crucified Jesus, they did not keep in mind the power of God.

"When the disciples dismissed the women's report of the resurrection as an idle tale, they did not keep in mind the power of God."

With every sentence, the distant trumpets in Isaiah's voice came closer and closer: "Before you ask, 'Can God spread a table in the wilderness?' keep in mind the power of God."

Members of the congregation began to answer the trumpets with their own trumpets: "Amen!" "Amen!" Every time Isaiah returned to the phrase "keep in mind the power of God," some of the congregation echoed back to him: "Keep in mind the power of God."

"When the power of doubt starts to overtake the power of faith, keep in mind the power of God. When the power of hate begins to overcome the power of love, keep in mind the power of God. When the power of despair attacks the power of hope, keep in mind the power of God.

"When you ask, 'Can God spread a table in the wilderness?' keep in mind the power of God.

"When people treat you like a nobody, keep in mind the power of God, the God whose image you bear and whose strength gives you strength.

"When you wonder if it matters to stand up for justice against the powers of injustice, keep in mind the power of God; keep in mind the power that defeated Pharaoh's army; keep in mind the power that rolled away the stone and raised our precious Savior from death.

"When you ask, 'Can God spread a table in the wilderness?' keep in mind the power of God. Keep in mind the disciples on the road to Emmaus.

"In their wilderness of grief, God spread a table—a table where the risen Christ was their host, a table where they were raised to new life, a table where people come from north and south and east and west, a table where all God's children are welcome, a table where God will wipe away every tear and there will be no more weeping and crying.

"When you ask, 'Can God spread a table in the wilderness?' keep in mind the power of God.

"Keep in mind the power of God, and the power of God will

give you power—power to love and power to heal, power to preach and power to feed, power to stand for justice and power to resist evil.

"Can God spread a table in the wilderness? Keep in mind the power of God." The joy and faith in Isaiah's voice and face were contagious.[15] Even members of the congregation who were not used to responding orally to a preacher found themselves answering Isaiah aloud.

The sermon had started with exhaustion in the wilderness, but by the time it was over, the congregation had feasted on the power of God. The results of the meal poured into their conversation about the sermon afterwards.

People explained why Isaiah Thompson's sermon lifted them up and empowered them. For some it was the way Isaiah had named the wilderness of their own lives; for others it was the breadth of his biblical vision; and for all of them it was the manner in which Isaiah embodied the conviction he proclaimed.

But none of these explanations nor all of them together were quite satisfactory to Roger Hawkins, the pastor from Grafton Heights. All he could say was "At the end I realized that Isaiah had spoken about many of the great issues of our nation—street people, lack of food, spiritual hunger—but I never felt overwhelmed by these things, as I do in so many sermons. I walked out of the chapel back to this seminar room with a more buoyant step, almost forgetting that I had recently gotten off crutches for my sprained ankle.

"I think of how my wife responds when I preach on big social themes. Alice believes these topics belong in the pulpit. But often when I finish, she says she goes out more burdened than when she came in."

Several members of the class acknowledged that they felt the same way about their own preaching or preaching that they had heard others do.

Peter Linden suggested that the power of Isaiah's sermon lay in what Henry Mitchell calls "the sermon celebration." "Mitchell reminds us," said Peter, "that 'people *do* what they *celebrate*,'[16] especially when their celebration 'expresses gladness about what God has done and is doing.'[17] God does not give us instructions and then leave us on our own. God works with us. Isaiah did far more than tell us about God's power. He led us into a celebration of that power so that we could feel the joy and the strength of it in our own lives. When we celebrate God's presence and activity we receive strength. As Roger put it, our step becomes more buoyant. The physical response is evidence of what has happened in the depths of the heart."

While Peter Linden spoke, he noticed that Roger Hawkins was no longer looking quite so buoyant. Roger explained: "I'm realizing that I've got to rewrite my sermon for Sunday. It's the same one I'm doing for class next week. I thought it was finished. But now I see that all it really does is put another burden on the congregation. There's no celebration in it."

The way Roger Hawkins developed his insight about sermon celebration was a model of how preachers can learn from one another across the boundaries of tradition and culture. Roger Hawkins did not imitate or try to sound like Isaiah Thompson. Instead, Roger adapted the principle of celebration to his own voice in the pulpit. And he did it with a biblical text that challenged his ability to the fullest.

Romans 12 is one exhortation after another: "Outdo one another in showing honor. Do not lag in zeal, be ardent in spirit, serve the Lord. Rejoice in hope, be patient in suffering, persevere in prayer." It was a passage that Peter Linden dreaded to hear from the pulpit, for in his experience, most of the sermons that Romans 12 inspired left listeners reeling in their pews, like soldiers in a bunker after heavy bombardment.

That was the kind of sermon Roger Hawkins had originally planned to preach. But then he experienced Isaiah Thompson's homiletical celebration, and Roger entirely rewrote his sermon.

Unlike Isaiah, Roger was a manuscript preacher, but very skillful at it. He used an oral form of writing, arranging his sentences on paper the way he wanted to speak them, not in paragraphs of prose, but in lines of varying length.

Peter Linden used to have a full copy of Roger's sermon, but all he could find in his file were the first two pages. His eyes moved easily down the beginning of the manuscript, which featured as much white space as print. Because the manuscript represented the patterns of Roger's speech, it was easy for Peter to hear him again in his memory. Although the trumpets that had echoed in Isaiah's delivery played more softly in Roger's voice, they still sounded a clear call to a new way of life. Roger began the sermon with a happy announcement:

The church has received a letter informing us of a fabulous bequest.

I know we've often grumbled that we don't have enough resources to be doing all that we should.

But this letter makes it clear: we can spend everything we have because there's plenty more to come.

I read a little bit from the letter this morning, the verses from Romans 12.

That's the part that encourages our extravagance: ". . . love one another with mutual affection; outdo one another in showing honor. Do not lag in zeal, be ardent in spirit, serve the Lord. Rejoice in hope, be patient in suffering, persevere in prayer. Contribute to the needs of the saints; extend hospitality to strangers."

Who has time or energy to do all that?

I wonder if Paul would change his tune

if he had to pick up one child at practice,

take another to the dentist,

rush home to get supper,

change the laundry and get out to the PTA meeting.

Paul urges an expenditure of love that seems far beyond our resources.

He sounds unrealistic—until we go back and read the first half of the letter, which tells us about the bequest.

I suspect that most of us, if we inherited a large fortune, would spend a modest amount of it on a few of our favorite dreams.

But then we would invest the major portion in some secure and dependable fund.

Our minds might tell us we were wealthy, but our hearts would still keep track of every cent.

And it's the same way with love,

the same way with grace,

the same way with forgiveness and patience.

Paul writes to remind us just how wealthy God's generosity has made us.

There's no need to skimp on love because under the terms of the bequest "God's love has flooded our hearts."

We can throw out the ledger books on revenge because Christ has done the same for us. "While we were yet sinners Christ died for us."

We can persist in prayer until when we run out of words and tears, because the Spirit continues praying for us "in sighs too deep for words."

We can love and pray and forgive extravagantly because God is extravagant to us.

Richard Meux Benson, who founded the Society of St. John the Evangelist in 1866, tells us one way to draw on the riches God has given us through Christ. He writes:

"There is within us a depth, not of our heart, but deeper than our heart. If we enter into ourselves we shall find the ground of our heart as it were broken up, and a deep well springing up from beneath it. There we find admission into the Being of God."[18]

And having been admitted there, we do not despair, but we thrill to hear Paul say:

". . . love one another with mutual affection; outdo one another in showing honor. Do not lag in zeal, be ardent in spirit, serve the Lord. Rejoice in hope, be patient in suffering, persevere in prayer."

Instead of feeling burdened by these words, we are delighted and empowered, for they remind us of the fabulous bequest that is ours through Jesus Christ.

That was as much of Roger Hawkins's manuscript as Peter Linden still had in his file. But Peter remembered that the rest of the sermon was a take-off on a popular television commercial for the state lottery. The commercial featured various working and middle-class people, with each saying what he or she would do with the multimillion dollar jackpot.

"I'd cruise around the world."

"I'd buy out my boss."

"I'd take a safari through Africa."

"I'd buy a private mountain lake."

After the statement of each dream there was a scene that lasted three to four seconds, showing the winner enjoying his or her fantasy, as if each had chosen the winning number.

Roger Hawkins rewrote the commercial for his sermon. He pictured the Grafton Heights church living in complete confidence that Paul's claims about the love of God were true. What had seemed a litany of impossible commandments when he first read them from Romans 12 became a vision of the church spending God's love on the world with the same extravagance as Christ.

Roger's voice took on a buoyancy that in its own way was as empowering as Isaiah Thompson's "keep in mind the power of God."

Roger preached the sermon first at his church, then in class. During the seminar discussion, he reported that Alice, his wife, and many others in Grafton Heights felt lifted up and inspired by the sermon.

Alice had been particularly fond of the quotation from Richard Meux Benson. She pointed out that Roger often attacked people's propensity to look inward, assuming it was an act of narcissism. But in fact it was for her and many others a way of doing exactly what Benson said: finding the depth that is "deeper than our heart," a way of entering into the presence of God.

Alice had recently joined a prayer circle that was reading the book *Prayer and Temperament: Different Forms of Prayer for Different Personality Types.* The authors had affirmed the principle that while we may "prefer the type of prayer that matches our natural temperament, we should familiarize ourselves with the other forms of prayer."[19]

Moved by Roger's sermon, Alice suggested that if preachers expanded their range of spiritual expression beyond their personality types, then listeners would do the same. Preaching would remind the church that the character of God is richer than any one personality type. "Then everyone," Alice said, "might feel welcome at the church's celebration."

Not all of the congregation in Grafton Heights shared Alice's excitement over Roger's sermon on the fabulous bequest of Christ. One of the trustees, while shaking Roger's hand at the door, warned: "Your sermon represents a dangerous pattern of thought that's landed this country in terrible trouble. There's no free lunch. You can't spend what you don't have, and you don't have what you don't earn."

By the time Roger shared the trustee's response with the class, he was less hurt than he was puzzled. Why did the man not want to join in the celebration of grace?

"Because," said Isaiah Thompson, "the man is right. Your sermon does represent 'a dangerous pattern of thought.' The extravagant love of God is a danger to the human illusion that we have earned whatever is ours, whether it's the love of our friends or the land that we own or the reserve in our bank account.

"I've always been amused by people who tell preachers to stay out of politics and stick with something safe like the grace of God. Nothing in the world is more dangerous than grace. Once you realize the only reason your heart is beating is because of God's grace, then you begin to see that everything good is a gift, and that loosens up the whole world.

"Your celebration of grace was loosening up that trustee's world, and he didn't want it to come loose. I'll say this for the man: I think he was a good listener. He let you know he was angry, and people don't get angry like that unless you step on something important to them. If you want to know about the challenge of preaching the gospel into the twenty-first century, I doubt that you can do much better than talking with somebody who gets upset at the idea of the grace of God."

As Isaiah Thompson finished speaking, Roger Hawkins looked across the table and said: "I had been so excited by the celebration in your sermon and the way it inspired me to rewrite my own sermon. It made a great difference to Alice and to many others. But I guess I had hoped it would work for everyone."

"Nothing ever works for everyone in the pulpit," observed Peter Linden.

"Celebration doesn't work for everyone in my church," admitted Isaiah. "It doesn't work for everyone in the Gospels either. Think of all the people who excuse themselves from the wedding feast."

"I know you're right," said Roger Hawkins. Then he let out a hard sigh, and the tone of his voice revealed that the trustee's response still weighed upon him. "But when the celebration of God's grace draws nothing but resistance, what are we preachers supposed to do?"

Several of the class members looked directly at Roger and said in unison: "Keep in mind the power of God."

Chapter 4

The Voice Upon the Deep

Hearing Christ in Unexpected Ways

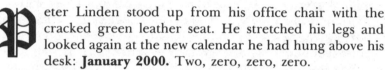eter Linden stood up from his office chair with the cracked green leather seat. He stretched his legs and looked again at the new calendar he had hung above his desk: **January 2000.** Two, zero, zero, zero.

The appearance of the number reminded him of when he was a child riding in the front seat of the car and his father alerted him that the odometer was about to turn over a new thousand miles. Peter fixed his eyes on the gauge as though the car were passing into some fabled land with the magic wholeness of the number. And then a mile later it was all forgotten as the back seat continued to squeak when they hit a bump or his father veered to avoid a pothole.

Peter wondered if it would not be the same now that the twenty-first century was here, a rustle of excitement at the clean new number on the calendar, but soon the same old bumps and squeaks in every realm of life, including preaching.

January 2000.

Peter walked over to the window and looked toward the blue hills that rose south of the city. He thought of Indian Mound Road and Clydes Corners some fifty miles away, and his heart picked up as he remembered a letter that Jason Kirk sent him upon his retirement in 1995. Peter had saved the letter in the course file, and he pulled it out, sat down in his chair, and reread what he affectionately called "The Epistle of St. Jason Kirk to Peter Linden."

Dear Peter,

It looks as though I will not be preaching the gospel into the 21st century, except for occasional Sundays when I supply the pulpit. I decided last year when I turned 70 that it was time to retire.

One of the luxuries of my increased leisure is that I find myself writing the letters I always wanted to write but never did. I think the letters are as much for me as they are for the people to whom I send them. They are a way of putting my life into perspective, a way of bringing closure to my ministry.

I still remember ''Preachers in Search of Their Voices,'' including the opening class when you asked us to recount our best memory of a sermon or preacher that had a positive impact upon our life. If I were to repeat that exercise today, I would name not one preacher, but all the preachers in the course, because the most valuable thing was the impact of hearing so many different voices in the pulpit. I still take issue with a lot of their theology. But if I were starting my ministry now, or if I had many years yet to preach before me, I would seek out such a group. It struck me after the class was over that out of all the things we ministers do, we seldom feed each other on the Word of God.

Those preachers awakened new visions in me, including a vision of how to solve the conflict in the Clydes Corners church. If the course were still meeting, I have a sermon I would be eager to preach.

I would begin by telling the class how their preaching loosened the rigidities of my own thought. Their faith challenged my faith until I started thinking in new ways about everything in my life, including that couch. I figured that if we can move the theological furniture in our minds, we can move the furniture in the chancel, and that's exactly what we did in Clydes Corners.

First, I got everybody in the congregation to agree that we needed to refurnish the church parlor. I suggested a historical motif, along the

93

lines of the seminar room where we met on campus. I pointed out that Cedric's couch was coming unglued and the veneers were splitting because of the extreme changes of temperature in the sanctuary, which during the winter we bring up to room temperature only on Sunday mornings. I thought we could have the couch repaired and then placed in the parlor, which we keep at room temperature all week because some group or committee meets there nearly every day. Folks who missed Sunday would still see Cedric's couch on weekdays.

All of Cedric's relatives agreed, and the new people helped put up money for the entire project, including the cost of framing a portrait of Cedric Clyde to hang over his couch. We also framed the charter for the church, which bears Cedric's scrawling signature, and several photographs of the early days of settlement.

I noticed in the background of one of these pictures some of the Indian mounds that Dorian White Elk had asked about. Every time I look at that photograph, I hear Dorian's soft voice returning to me and telling the class: ''This is the task of proclaiming the gospel into the 21st century: to raise from oblivion the people who have been plowed over.'' I did not manage to do that in the last years of my ministry, but I pray to God the next generation of preachers will.

When all the redecorating was completed, the congregation gathered one Sunday in the parlor for a dedication. I said a prayer, and Florence Clyde, the oldest living member of the Clyde family, unveiled the plaque on the parlor door, which read:

The Cedric Clyde Memorial Parlor
Refurnished to the Glory of God
and in honor of Cedric Clyde,
beloved husband, father and community leader
and founder and benefactor of this church.

94

Then we processed to the sanctuary. I remember looking at the couch as we marched out of the parlor and thinking how that antique piece required a protected environment of constant temperature to keep from falling apart. I thought of ''Preachers in Search of Their Voices'' and the way I struggled with nearly every new idea in order to protect the theology of my early years. I realized then that I had been like the Clyde family, protecting my version of the faith as vehemently as the Clydes had protected their couch.

I stayed in the course because I wanted a faith sturdier than that antique sofa. I wanted a faith that did not need a controlled environment in order to survive, a faith that could endure the extremes of the world.

When we processed from the parlor into the sanctuary, we all gathered up front to dedicate the new furnishings in the chancel. We had hung a large cross on the wall behind the pulpit, and where the couch used to sit there were now two chairs with the same simple lines as the rest of the church.

I preached a sermon on the cross that day, which was well received by everyone. Isaiah Thompson's mother and Chung Won Kim's family were among my illustrations of people who daily took up their crosses to follow Jesus. Several people said it was like fresh air to hear about these individuals outside of our little church. I'm sure the comment was in part a reflection of the upbeat tone of the whole day, but it made me think of your vision, ''heart—deep and world wide.'' Maybe your vision is possible even in a place like Clydes Corners.

If this story were a sermon for the class, my text would be the parable of the evil spirits in Matthew. The lesson begins with a single bad spirit that is driven out of someone. The spirit wanders over desolate places and later returns to find the person's life orderly but empty. So the spirit gathers seven other bad spirits and invites them to take residence in the neat but empty rooms of the person's soul.

I could never say this directly to the people in Clydes Corners, but that is what we did when we took the old couch out of the chancel: we drove the bad spirit out, and the cross and the new chairs brought a new spirit in. If we had not made plans for the cross and the chairs, the whole thing could have backfired. We might have gotten the couch into the parlor, but in a week or so, I suspect, the Clydes would have found some other piece just as ugly, something they had stored in one of their barns or attics. I did not let that couch out of the chancel until the parcel service delivered the cross and the chairs.

Maybe that is why I was so resistant to the sermons in class that called for radical reinterpretations of the Christian faith. I feared the preachers were throwing out tradition and creating a spiritual vacuum, and the next thing would be bad spirits rushing in to take over.[1] Tashika, Dorian, and Marjorie were able to see things that eluded my vision, and so I had to hang on with the same stubbornness as the Clydes hung on to the couch in the chancel.

But having seen the change in Clydes Corners, I have begun to think there are many ways for Christ to drive out the bad spirits and to replace them with the wholeness that is our salvation.

When I read all this to Gladys, my wife, she went over to the piano and opened the hymn book, and asked me to sing the hymn we sang when Katherine Carr preached on one of the exorcism texts from the Gospels.

Peter Linden put down Jason's letter, and his head filled with the driving beat of "Silence, Frenzied, Unclean Spirit," and snatches of verses that pounded in his heart:

"Silence, frenzied, unclean spirit!"
cried God's healing Holy One. . . .
Lord, the demons still are thriving
in the gray cells of the mind:
tyrant voices, shrill and driving,
twisted thoughts that grip and bind. . . .
Silence, Lord, the unclean spirit
in our mind and in our heart.[2]

Peter returned to Jason Kirk's letter and found Jason quoting the hymn's final lines, which had escaped his own memory:

''By the power of your healing make us faithful, true and whole.'' That's the prayer I would offer at the end of this sermon, if I were to preach it to the members of the class. It would be a prayer to silence the unclean spirit, a prayer to be filled with the power that makes us ''faithful, true, and whole.''

I am sending a copy of this letter to all the other members of the class. I got their addresses from the dean's office because I want them to know that even though my vision was not always the same as theirs, still I heard in their voices the sighs of the Spirit that are too deep for words. I continue praying for them and for their preaching. I do not pray that they preach as I would but that they may faithfully speak the vision which the Spirit gives them, a vision that I finally have enough grace to realize will probably be far different and far greater than the imaginings of my heart.

I'm as healthy as ever, but a little slower getting around. I probably will make it past the year 2000 before I slip away for good. I never have speculated too much on what that will be like. I simply trust that what Paul says is true: Nothing in all of creation, not even death, can separate us from the love of God in Christ Jesus our Lord.

That belief has saved me again and again when the demons have risen in my own heart. And should fear

overtake me at the end, I shall speak those words to
the very face of death and be at peace.

All the best to you,

Jason Kirk

Peter Linden put down Jason's letter and started tracing the
outline of the blue hills in the distance. On an early Sunday
morning in June of 1990, after the course was over, Peter drove
down to Clydes Corners to hear Jason preach and to see with his
own eyes the famous couch, which at that time was still in the
chancel.

The memory of that giant ugly sofa was enough to stir in Peter
a new appreciation for the puritan instinct to remove everything
from the church that would block a clear and single focus on God.
Peter thought of all the monstrous theological furniture that had
cluttered the church through the ages, its anti-Semitism and
racism, its violence, its sexism, its homophobia, its condescending
treatment of people with disabling conditions.

The thought of all these different "isms" brought to Peter's
memory Eddie Hanson's sermon, "Christianity Is Not Christianism." It was the boldest statement Eddie ever made to the class
about the theology of his holiness tradition. Perhaps he spoke so
plainly because it was near the end of the term, or perhaps
because he had been accepted at the prestigious graduate school
of his choice, and this had affirmed his intellectual excellence in
the eyes of his peers and boosted his self-confidence when he was
around them. Or perhaps it was simply, as Eddie himself said,
"because the Holy Spirit has laid this message upon my heart."

Peter remembered how Eddie's three-point sermon was
arranged to follow the storyline from Acts 2:

1. The world does not understand the Holy Spirit.
2. The world does not control the Holy Spirit.
3. The world is called to repent by the Holy Spirit.

Eddie started the sermon with verses 12 and 13: "All were
amazed and perplexed, saying to one another, 'What does this
mean?' But others sneered and said, 'They are filled with new
wine.' "

Eddie drew a parallel between the baffled response to the first Pentecost and the continuing inability of the world to understand the anointing of the Holy Spirit and the blessing of holiness. He pointed out that when the apostle Peter explained the impact of the wind and fire of the Holy Spirit, he did not appeal to the immediate world of his listeners but to a prophecy from Joel.

"Peter did not reduce the gifts of the Holy Spirit to the 'isms' of this world," said Eddie. Then he told how the conversations in class, and indeed his whole seminary education, felt to him like an attempt to reverse the process, to let the "isms" of this world define who the Holy Spirit is and to control how the Holy Spirit works.

"Christianity is not Christianism. It's not feminism or liberalism or conservatism. It's responding to the work of the Holy Spirit, who draws us to Christ and to a life of holiness.

"We need to experience again what the listeners to Peter's sermon felt: 'They were cut to the heart and said to Peter and the rest of the apostles, "Brethren, what shall we do?" And Peter said to them, "Repent, and be baptized every one of you in the name of Jesus Christ for the forgiveness of your sins; and you shall receive the gift of the Holy Spirit." ' "

Eddie illustrated his points with a story about a man named Karl, who was a next-door neighbor when Eddie was growing up. When Karl had too much to drink, he sometimes brought out a gun at night and shot it into the sky, waking up the neighbors. When he saw people looking from their windows he would threaten to shoot them, and they often called the cops, who would come and get him to put down the gun and then carry him off to jail. But he had never actually shot at anybody, and he was never in jail for long.

The police called in a psychiatric social worker on the case, but he had absolutely no influence on Karl. A number of neighbors purchased guns and threatened that the next time Karl started shooting, they would shoot him in self-defense.

Eddie's father began preaching to Karl. At first it had no effect whatsoever. But when Karl's left hand got mangled in a machine in the defense plant where he worked with Eddie's father, it was Mr. Hanson who drove him to the hospital and helped him fill out the union medical forms and later picked up his prescription and brought him groceries. As a result of all this, Karl went to church one Sunday with the Hansons.

"And while Karl was in church—I still remember the day," said Eddie, "the power of the Holy Spirit came from on high and anointed him, and he was 'cut to the heart' and repented and was baptized.

"Afterwards, the social worker, who had been a complete failure with Karl, suggested the man was having some kind of psychological breakdown. That was the only way he could make sense of Karl's new talk about 'the unction of the Holy Spirit' and 'the healing blessings' that had come to him. Most of the neighbors did not understand what had happened either, but they were so glad the nights were no longer filled with gunshots that they just let things be.

"As I said at the beginning:
The world does not understand the Holy Spirit.
The world does not control the Holy Spirit.
The world is called to repent by the Holy Spirit."

The conversation that followed Eddie's sermon was one of the most convoluted of the entire class. Peter thought the other students would challenge Eddie for disparaging what he had called their "isms," but they did not. Their first responses were reserved and guarded. Perhaps they realized how much Eddie had risked himself after having been so quiet throughout the term. Or perhaps their initial tentativeness reflected what Katherine Carr said: "I felt as you spoke that you were saying something important, something that puts in a different light all that we have been talking about in this class. But at the same time I could not really enter the sermon because as much as you treasure that language about the Holy Spirit, I need more ways of talking about what it means."

After Katherine spoke, many others made similar responses, and from then on the conversation became more and more entangled as the students kept trying to use their academic theological terms to try to understand the vocabulary of Eddie's pentecostal holiness tradition. Eddie told them their attempts were "reductionistic, illustrating exactly what my sermon says: the world does not understand the Holy Spirit."

The students responded that Eddie's way of preaching sounded like going around in circles to them.

The total effect of the conversation was like foreigners speaking to one another, each knowing something of the other's language but not enough to enter fully into the other's world.

At the end of class, however, several students thanked Eddie for his sermon. He had communicated to them the sovereignty of the Holy Spirit and the danger of overidentifying the gospel with their own causes. He also had done something else for them: His insistence that the language of his tradition could not be translated into their way of talking made them aware that there were limits to their openness and inclusivity, which they had not previously acknowledged.

As Peter recalled the verbal entanglements between Eddie and the class, he could hear Dorian White Elk telling about his grandmother who was never converted by the missionaries because, as she said: "All those Christians do is quarrel with each other about the meaning of their Book. They claim the Book is about God and love. Well, I say, let them start living what the Book says, and then maybe I'll get interested."

Dorian White Elk's sermon was titled "Get Your Nose Out of the Book."

He began with a saying that was common among American Indians: "When the missionaries arrived, 'they had only the Book and we had the land; now we have the Book and they have the land.' "[3]

"Christians took our land of forests," said Dorian, "and gave us a forest of words." His voice was as soft in the pulpit as it was at the seminar table. "They took our land filled with the song of the bird and gave us the hymns of a distant promised land. They took the mountains that were holy to us and gave us the mountain of Zion. They took the wilderness where we lived and told us the stories of the wilderness of Sinai.

"They took the land. We got the Book.

"And there are many now who want to reverse the exchange. They are my brothers and sisters, and if they were here in this pulpit they would tell you: 'Take back your Book and return the land to us. If you must live in a forest, live in the forest of your words. But let us listen to the night with the call of the bird and the silence of the stars. Drink from the streams of Zion all you want, but leave our streams alone, pure and clear, free of the waste of your wasteful living.' "

Then Dorian spoke for himself instead of his sisters and brothers. He picked up the Bible and said: "I love the Book for telling me about Jesus, my friend, my teacher, my guide."

With these words of personal testimony, Dorian fell silent, and the sermon came to a complete stop as he gazed out the chapel window to the side of the pulpit. Dorian's eyes traced the clump of cedars outside on the lawn and beyond them the horizon of hills. The class could see his eyes scanning the whole scene. With the sweep of his arm Dorian invited them to look outside. One by one the listeners turned their gaze from the pulpit to the windows. The silence continued for a long time.

Finally, Dorian said: "I love the land as much as I love the Book. I love the land that breathes with the wind that breathed on my ancestors."

He explained that there were places in the land that were as sacred to him as passages from the Bible.

"There was a creek near my grandmother's house, where I used to spend the summers when I was a little boy. The creek came down between two ridges of high steep hills with scattered pines and sharp outcroppings of rock.

"My grandmother used to go down to that creek at the dawn of each day to comb out her hair and to pray. I woke to the sound of her high voice fluttering on the air, echoing off the stone of the ridges.

"I would get out of bed and run to my grandmother. Only the brightest stars remained in the sky. I would sit on the flat rock at the stream's edge and listen to my grandmother, blending her voice with the birds in praise of the creator spirit. Then she would fall silent till the loudest sound was the song of the stream.

"The sun's rays broke across the top of the eastern hills and gilded the rim of the western ridge. Then, as the sun rose higher, the shadow of the eastern hills moved down the slopes of the western ridge. If you were perfectly still and fixed your eye on a large boulder or a lone tree, you could see the line of the shadow moving downward as the sun climbed into the sky. My grandmother said, 'The sun is drawing back the blanket of night to wake up the children of earth.'

"Every evening we returned to the same flat stone by the stream, this time to watch the shadow of the western ridge climb up the eastern hills as the sun sank down and the blanket of night was spread over us again.

"I remember, one evening, we were stepping out the door to go down to the creek. My mother was by the window, reading the

Bible in the slanted light. My grandmother, who never attacked my mother for becoming Christian, said to her on this occasion: 'Sometimes even Christians need to get their nose out of the Book. Instead of reading the Book, they need to read the land. Come on down to the creek with us.' My mother came along, and I remember sitting quietly between the two of them, and as I watched the shadow climb up the mountain, I thought to myself, 'I'm reading the land.'

"My grandmother is dead now, but when I toss and turn in bed, I take myself back to the flat rock by the stream and join her again. Together we watch the blanket of night spread over the valley. I read the land, peace descends, and I sleep.

"Sometimes when I bog down in theology, I hear my grandmother saying to me: 'Get your nose out of the Book and read the land.'

"That's why I had you gaze for a long time at the clump of cedars and the horizon of the hills. I wanted you to read the land. The problem with people of the Book is that they think they have trapped the world in their words. But speaking the word *land* does not bring the smell of soil to your nostrils or the darkness of the cedars to your eyes.

"Get your nose out of the Book and read the land. Read the deep and holy silence of the land. Read the dawn light, read the shadow on the hills, read the shape of rock and tree against the sky. Read the fingerprints of God in the land. Read the land.

"Get your nose out of the Book and read the land. Read not only its beauty, but also the scars and wounds we have inflicted on the land. Get your nose out of the Book and read the land. And, in the deep and holy silence of your reading, you will find a new voice for preaching the gospel into the twenty-first century. Get your nose out of the Book and read the land."

When Dorian had finished his sermon in the chapel, the class members did not get out of their pews to leave for the seminar room as they usually did. Instead, all of them found themselves gazing out the window, reading the land, reading the clump of cedars and the horizon of the hills beyond the campus, the same cedars and the same hills that Peter was now reading from his office window as he remembered the sermon ten years later.

Peter recalled the class discussion after the sermon. It had felt entirely different from any of the other discussions. The effect of

Dorian's subdued delivery and his long silence, allowing people to look out the window, had permeated each listener. Instead of debating the sermon, the class shared memories of favorite trees and streams, some of them in the country, some of them in city parks, the haunts of their childhoods evoked by Dorian's story.

The discussion sounded more like talk around a campfire than conversation around a seminar table. Dorian White Elk had awakened the voice of the land in the people of the Book. Describing rock and sky, the preachers talked with a refreshing simplicity. They spoke from a level of reality that for too long had been buried beneath layers of theological encrustation.

But an entirely different kind of discussion followed Tashika Bronson's sermon on the atonement. If Dorian White Elk's grandmother had heard the uproar over Tashika's sermon, it would only have confirmed her opinion that "all those Christians do is quarrel with each other about the meaning of their Book."

It was Tashika's sermon more than any other that made Jason Kirk write in his letter: "my vision was not always the same as" those of the other students. And it was Tashika who responded to Jason with a letter of her own, which she also sent to everyone who had taken the course.

Peter kept the two letters together in his file as a witness that Christians with opposing theologies can still maintain their relationship with each other. Whenever Peter read the letters in tandem, it made him think of how the Bible itself is filled with a plurality of voices. The canon is a collection of diversity, not uniformity. Peter viewed the contradictions and incongruities of Scripture as a symbol of the dynamic character of faith, as a reminder that God lives more comfortably with ambiguity than humans do. All of this suggested to Peter that the church is most biblical when it allows for a multitude of voices.

Peter felt the tension of listening to those voices as he began to read once again what he affectionately called "The Epistle of St. Tashika Bronson to the Church That Once Gathered as Preachers in Search of Their Voices."

Dear Friends,

I know Jason has sent all of us a copy of his letter to Peter, and I want to thank Jason for writing and for offering prayers on our behalf.

I am especially touched, Jason, by your statement that you do not pray that we will preach as you would, but you ask instead that we will be faithful to the vision the Spirit gives us.

Like you, Jason, I am writing this letter as a way of writing to myself, because I still remember the severity of our disagreement after I preached my sermon titled ''Cross of Love, Cross of Hate.''

In the beginning of the sermon I told about watching a morning news report on the bombing of Baghdad. There were pictures of our forces loading so-called smart bombs and missiles underneath the wings of our planes. I watched a soldier draw a cross on one of the bombs and write beside it the words: ''Mr. Hussein, if calling on Allah doesn't work, try Jesus Christ.'' The next thing I saw were night shots of Baghdad in flames. I wondered in terror: Where had the cross exploded?

Chung Won and Jason, both of you told me during the class discussion that you had been with me all the way in the first part of the sermon. You each had suffered through a war, and you were horrified at the appeal to Christ to justify destruction.

I tried in my sermon to figure out how the cross, the symbol of forgiveness and reconciliation, could be used for the exact opposite, for tearing apart and roasting human flesh. I asked: ''Why does the cross become a weapon? Why does the cross of love become the cross of hate?'' That has got to be a central question for people who are finding their voices to preach the gospel into the 21st century.

I started with an orthodox answer: Human sin is so deep we can distort anything, even a symbol of salvation.

Then I turned from that standard theological explanation to suggest that the root of the problem lies in the doctrine of atonement.[4] I recall seeing many of your faces cloud over as I preached this from the pulpit.

I repeated what Dorian said in his sermon: ''The

105

problem with the people of the Book is they think
they have trapped the world in their words.'' I
thought of the countless hymns and sermons I had
heard on the atonement of Christ, and I realized
that all those words had not trapped the meaning of
Christ's death. They had trapped something else
instead: an understanding of God that supports the
violence in the human heart, an understanding that
would lead someone to draw the cross of Jesus on a
bomb.

Why does the cross of love become the cross of
hate?

I stand even more strongly today behind the
answer I gave then: The cross of love becomes the
cross of hate because of the way the church has
often preached about the cross. To say that Jesus
had to die for our sins is to reinforce violence and
retribution as divinely ordained. It is to confirm
in the religious imagination that God is an
abusive father.

If atonement means that God required Jesus'
death, then atonement is heresy to the gospel of
our Savior, heresy to the gospel of reconciliation, heresy to the gospel of grace.

As Peter read Tashika's words in silence, he could hear her
voice and picture her speaking the letter with the same conviction
that marked the delivery of her sermon and the defense of her
ideas during the class discussion.

Her letter continued:

I told in the sermon how my father used to knock
around my deaf brother, Darryl, especially when
Darryl did wrong, and my father, out of frustration
at being unable to communicate, would shake him
violently by the arms and throw him to the ground.

I remember the day I came home and found Darryl
crying in his room after some Christian, who had
learned to sign so he could preach good news to the
deaf, claimed that God required the death of his Son

for our forgiveness. Darryl had made an instant connection between that sermon and Dad's violence.

All of you were sensitive to my feelings for my brother, but some of you said that such personal stories are not adequate for a critique of atonement. I still disagree with you about that. I believe, if a doctrine is horrifying to a deaf and battered child, then it's not the gospel. If we pile theological arguments from hell to heaven to justify a doctrine and it still leaves the heart of a child trembling in fear, then we know it's heresy in the eyes of our Savior, who himself said: ''It would be better for you if a millstone were hung around your neck and you were thrown into the sea than for you to cause one of these little ones to stumble'' (Luke 17:2).

You wanted more examples, something greater than my family situation, before you were convinced that the violent use of the cross arises from our interpretation of the cross. I regret to say I am gathering more of them all the time.

Last year I attended a session of the state legislature, which was considering the reinstitution of the death penalty. Several of those who were in favor of it, including a state senator, specifically appealed to God's sacrifice of Jesus as the divine sanction of public execution.

I have several times talked with a counselor who works with abusive husbands and fathers. He has told me of abusers who have justified their violence by appealing to what God the Father did to his Son.[5]

I know you would claim these are perversions of the cross, the devil using the sign of atonement for his own end. But my point still stands: Something is contorted in the way we preach and sing and pray about the cross. And if we are going to preach the gospel into the 21st century, then we have to figure out why the cross of love keeps getting used as the cross of hate.

107

Let me name a less dramatic example of the violence hidden in our understanding of Christ's atonement on the cross, an example that I could not see until after the course was over and I had more perspective. I write these next words in fear and trembling, but if I cannot write them, and if you cannot receive them, then there's no hope that we can stop the cross of love from becoming the cross of hate.

I'm thinking of the way you reacted in class to my sermon. I do not have in mind the fact that you disagreed with me. I expected that. After all, I was questioning a belief that was central and precious to several of you.

But what I was not prepared for was the raw anger in your voices. You said that Christ's sacrifice, his atoning death on the cross was ''necessary'' to make us more loving. But it seemed to me from the way you spoke that you were drawing more violence than love from the doctrine you were defending.

I do not believe for a moment that you did this deliberately because that is not in keeping with your character. Instead, I recall our painful conversation as an example of the tangled sin I was trying to get at in the sermon, the way that Christian belief can be enmeshed with the forces it purports to overcome.

And here I am willing to admit that my sermon may not have been as clear as I intended it to be.

What I am trying to say now is that the nature of your reaction to my sermon revealed what I was trying to communicate—namely, that atonement is a convoluted doctrine. It twists the gospel by making compassion and justice depend upon a god who contradicts those values. We cannot preach that God is love and in the same breath say that love demanded the death of an innocent victim.

I sometimes feel that we preachers are like sailors on a boat. In our hands is a lifeline that we need to throw to a world that is drowning. We are holding the rope in our hands, and we can feel the strands of hope, faith, and love that make the rope strong and resilient. But the rope has gotten tangled and twisted. Each of us is trying to get it straightened out, but we try to loosen the knots by pulling in opposite directions, and they only close tighter.

When I read your letter, Jason, I finally had an insight about why we pulled so violently in opposite directions that day in class. I am thinking of the part in your letter where you write:

> Maybe that is why I was so resistant to the sermons in class which called for radical reinterpretations of the Christian faith. I feared the preachers were throwing out tradition and creating a spiritual vacuum, and the next thing would be bad spirits rushing in to take over. Tashika, Dorian, and Marjorie were able to see things that eluded my vision, and so I had to hang on with the same stubbornness as the Clydes hung on to the couch in the chancel.

Your words make a lot of sense to me, Jason. Looking back at my sermon on atonement, I can see that I knew what I wanted to throw out, but I was not yet clear about what I wanted to bring in.

I wanted to throw out then, and I want to throw out now, the idea that there is a Father God who required the death of his Son. I want to throw out every twisted understanding of atonement that helps us turn the cross of love into the cross of hate. I want to throw out every perverted interpretation that leads someone to draw a cross on a bomb, to bruise a child, to batter a woman, to brutalize a gay person, to burn a cross in someone's yard.

But I want to do more than throw these things out. I want to replace them with a new definition of atonement. I've been doing some research, and I found a theological essay that's too technical for the pulpit but is good for feeding a preacher's thought.[6] The writer makes a lot of points, but the ones I remember are these:

1. Christian history reveals many interpretations of the cross, not just one.
2. We need to consider the societal forces that carried out the crucifixion.
3. The atoning work of Christ is not limited to the cross but includes his life, death, and resurrection as one coherent action.

The writer thinks of atonement as ''emancipatory solidarity.'' What he means by this is that we are liberated by Jesus' integrity, the integrity of his relationship to God and the integrity of his relationship to us. Tyrants hate such integrity because it shows them up for what they are and threatens their power.

God did not order the death of Jesus. Jesus was killed ''for being who he was,'' for doing what he preached, for living as a person of integrity.

''Emancipatory solidarity'' is the beginning of my new vision of atonement, flowing not only from the cross but from the entire life work of Jesus, his preaching and deeds as well as his death and resurrection. I have not yet translated the terms ''emancipatory solidarity'' into language for the pulpit, into stories that will make sense to people in the pew. But I am working on it.

If what I write here sounds inadequate or unsatisfying to you, Jason, I want you to keep praying for me anyway. I feel my thoughts are like the first day of creation; the Spirit has separated light and darkness, the waters above and below the firmament, but the Spirit has a lot more work yet to do. I want you to keep asking God that I will have the courage to preach the vision that the Spirit is continuing to create in me.

Whatever I end up preaching about the atonement

into the 21st century, I shall be praying with all
my heart a prayer that I know you, too, can pray in
good conscience: ''Dear Jesus, Precious Savior,
may your cross of love never again be used as the
cross of hate.''

Tashika Bronson

Peter put down the letter, and lines from hymns about the cross began to drift through his mind: "Jesus, keep me near the cross"; "Beneath the cross of Jesus, I fain would take my stand"; "In the cross of Christ I glory, towering o'er the wrecks of time." A melody began to sound in Peter's soul, and he started to sing, "When I Survey the Wondrous Cross." While his lips and vocal chords gave out the opening stanza, his heart was praying. "Dear Jesus, Precious Savior, may your cross of love never again be used as the cross of hate."

> When I survey the wondrous cross
> on which the Prince of Glory died,
> my richest gain I count but loss,
> and pour contempt on all my pride.

The hymn faded from Peter's mind, and he imagined the other members of the class receiving Tashika's letter in the mail and opening and reading it. If they were gathered together once again, would they be able to discuss Tashika's ideas more gracefully than they did that day in class? They had become friends during the course of the semester, but following the discussion of Tashika's sermon, they had all gotten up from the seminar table with shaking knees.

Karen Steel, who preached the next time the class met, acknowledged from the pulpit: "It was painful to experience last week in class the very thing that had discouraged Dorian's grandmother from even considering the gospel: 'All those Christians do is quarrel with each other about the meaning of their Book. They claim the Book is about God and love. Well I say, let them start living what the Book says, and then maybe I'll get interested.'"

Peter remembered that Karen had come by his office on several occasions to discuss how she was sometimes excited and

111

sometimes frustrated with the class. Those visits revealed bit by bit the pieces of Karen Steel's life, and they helped Peter to see that Karen's efforts to find a coherent "voice" in the pulpit were part of a larger personal struggle to make sense of her fragmented childhood.

Karen was born in 1967. Her mother had dropped out of high school to marry a boyfriend who had been drafted for service in Vietnam. Karen was conceived before he left, and she was born before he was due to return. But he died in action, and the only images Karen had of him were a few snapshots a friend had taken of the wedding and his senior class year book picture, which was autographed with a vow of eternal love to Karen's mother.

"That's why," said Karen, upon her first visit to Peter's office, "I get so still when Jason Kirk or Chung Won Kim speak in class. I can't get out of my mind: They've been there, they've been in war, like the war that killed my father; they've heard the shells, the mines explode. That second day when Chung Won said in class that he observed much suffering around the table, I almost got up and left in tears. I did not speak of my father's death because I knew it would overwhelm me. I had the same reaction when Tashika told about the cross drawn on the bomb. When does the suffering end?"

In a later conversation Karen told how her mother had worked as a typist/receptionist in an insurance agency until Karen was in third grade, when her mother remarried, this time to a sales representative for a major firm. They moved to a nice suburban house, and Karen thought it was going to be paradise. But her stepfather's job moved them around so much that she was never in one place for more than eighteen months.

"Wherever we moved," Karen said to Peter, "the first thing I always put out in my room was the miniature American flag my mother had waved toward my father as he boarded the plane for Vietnam. I would put the little stick the flag was on in a Coke bottle on my desk. And I always placed next to it a wallet-sized picture of Jesus that was given me for perfect attendance at vacation Bible school one summer. It was my own little altar where I would talk to Jesus and ask Jesus to talk to my father, who had last seen my mother when she was waving the flag and bearing me inside her."

One time when they moved while Karen was in fourth grade

they did not find the flag and the picture of Jesus when they unpacked. Karen had wept for several days, until her stepfather, who was usually patient with her, exploded: "For God's sake, child, it's just a little flag and picture. We can replace them."

Karen had shouted back. "No, you can't, you can't, you can't!"

The flag and picture finally turned up. One of the movers had rolled them inside a towel with some other odds and ends and stuffed them in the linen hamper. From that day on Karen never let any mover touch them. She always carried them to their new home on her own. And throughout her days in seminary they sat on her desk in the dormitory next to her Bible dictionaries and books of theology and pastoral care.

Karen began her last sermon with the story of the flag and picture of Jesus, and then she observed. "The turmoil of last week's class discussion about atonement brought back to me the panic I felt when I thought my little altar had been lost. As I come to the end of this course, I do not believe my story is all that uncommon. Each of us has some kind of altar in her or his heart, some symbol, some place or object or thought or doctrine that is our way to the Holy One. And when that altar is destroyed or lost, then we are shaken. We panic the same way I panicked as a child. We panic the same way that ancient Israel panicked in the face of the destruction of its holy places.

"You can hear the voice of panic in Psalm 11. The psalmist begins by questioning the advice of someone who counsels retreat in a time of conflict:

> In the LORD I take refuge; how
>   can you say to me,
> "Flee like a bird to the mountains . . . ?"

"The next verse describes the wicked getting ready to shoot the innocent with bow and arrow under the cover of night. The horror of it is not unlike what Jason told us about the exploding land mine, and what Marjorie told us about the battered woman, and what Chung Won told us about the soldiers firing at his family in the darkness.

"But the verse that haunts me most is the disparaging question that follows the scene of violence:

If the foundations are destroyed,
what can the righteous do?

"It may be that the foundations refer to the foundations of the temple. The voice that says, 'Flee like a bird to the mountains,' is the voice of one who fears the temple will fall, who fears that hostile forces will bring down the house of God, the house of truth and meaning.

"I believe that's the fear that set off my panic when the little flag and picture of Jesus were lost. I believe that's the fear that drove our debate about the cross and atonement. We felt as if the foundations were being destroyed, the foundations of the way we believe.

"I know what I did as the debate grew shrill. I started to withdraw. I listened to the voice that said: 'Flee like a bird to the mountains.' And I believe many of us preachers will do the same. We will flee by avoiding the kind of issues that Tashika dared to raise; we will flee from facing the violence and the distortions that are part of our own tradition. It is too painful to face up to.

"But the psalmist refuses to flee. The psalmist has a vision of God's temple that extends far beyond the dimensions of the earthly temple:

> The LORD is in his holy temple;
> the LORD's throne is in heaven.
> His eyes behold, his gaze
> examines humankind.

"Maybe the foundations of our human temple will be destroyed. Maybe the doctrines that we have so carefully quarried and smoothed to build our temple of meaning will give way. But the throne in heaven stands forever. God continues to watch us. God was guarding me even when I was in a panic over the loss of my little altar. God was looking at us all the time we were debating the atonement.

"Our security is not a temple built with human hands or human thought. Our security is not this doctrine or that. Our security is not a flag and a picture of Jesus. Our security is not even our theology. Our security is God, the truth of God, the being of God, the unblinking gaze of God.

The psalmist says:

114

The LORD tests the righteous and the wicked,
    and his soul hates the lover of violence.
On the wicked he will rain coals of fire and sulfur;
    a scorching wind shall be the portion of their cup.

"After listening to Tashika, I see in these verses what I never saw before. The God who hates violence is portrayed as a God who is violent: 'On the wicked he will rain coals of fire and sulfur.'

"I read those words, and I think of the soldier who drew the cross on the bomb and the pictures of Baghdad under attack, 'the coals of fire and sulfur' raining down.

"If we're going to preach the gospel into the twenty-first century, then we need to purify more than our understanding of the cross and atonement. We need to purify the way we imagine God.[7]

"I did not understand what Katherine meant at the start of this course when she said her goal for preaching into the twenty-first century was ' "the therapy of the religious imagination." ' But now I am beginning to see what that might mean. We have got to heal our imaginations of these ideas about God that are used to justify our ungodly terrors.

"I'm taking a course in church history this term, and it suggests just how broad and deep that 'therapy of the religious imagination' needs to go. Yesterday I read the opening essays in *The Oxford Illustrated History of Christianity*. The introduction to the volume widened last week's debate into realms we never touched. The editor, after quoting from one of Bonhoeffer's letters from prison, reflects:

> Perhaps the future of institutional Christianity, both in the relations of Christian bodies with each other, and in their relations with other religions and with the world, may be a sacrificial one, abandoning so much the past has cherished in striving to represent the Christ-like spirit. This idea is beginning in Christianity today, even in matters of doctrine, over which so much blood and ink has been spilt, and where assumptions of providential guidance have been so ruthlessly made.[8]

"Instead of spilling more blood and ink, we have to 'represent the Christ-like spirit.' The time of ruthlessly assuming providential guidance for all of our doctrines and positions is past. The way to

115

show the meaning of the cross and atonement is to *be* sacrificial, which means 'abandoning so much the past has cherished.'

"I am not sure that I have the courage to do this on my own. I believe that any preacher who dares to preach this way will be attacked as a heretic, one of those who is destroying the foundations.

"But I cannot get out of my mind that opening image from Tashika's sermon: the bomb with the cross and the words 'Mr. Hussein, if calling on Allah doesn't work, try Jesus Christ.' That bomb was dropped on people of another world religion, Islam.

"We will never stop such madness, if at the first shaking of the foundations we flee like a bird to the mountains, we flee to old-time religion, we flee to our own little cultural group.

"And we will only reinforce the madness if we insist that God is a God who showers down sulfur and coal. The world cannot afford to believe in God as a bombardier. That kind of belief will only provide divine sanction for the human terrors of war.

"When I think of the flag and the picture of Jesus at my little altar, my own sermon frightens me. It takes so much courage not to flee like a bird. But I believe God will give us that courage if we remember the best of the psalmist's vision: God's temple is not destroyed, even if ours is. God's gaze examines humankind. God is righteous, and the upright shall behold the face of God."

Peter Linden was not sure how the class would respond to Karen Steel's sermon. Since she had built on some of Tashika's controversial themes, he wondered if the class discussion would be as acrimonious as the week before. But Peter never found out what the class thought of Karen's sermon.

No sooner had they walked back from the chapel and sat down around the seminar table than Katherine Carr began to have contractions. Since this was not something that Peter Linden's Ph.D. in theology had prepared him for, he was glad that there was an experienced nurse present in the person of Marjorie Hudson. She took control as though she were back at her desk in the hospital.

"Roger, get your van and bring it around front. Karen, go get Katherine's coat from the women's lockers. Isaiah, go to the central office and have them call Katherine's husband to meet us at the hospital. Tashika, you walk with me and Katherine to the front door."

Then Marjorie put her arm around Katherine's shoulder, helped her up, and said: "You're doing fine, everything's going to be all right."

In no time they were out of the seminar room, and as the door shut behind them, the five remaining men—Dorian, Chung Won, Jason, Eddie, and Peter—fell quiet, as if some great intensity of life had swept through the room and then left for a territory to which they could never travel.

The only sound was the ticking of the old wall clock, which drew Peter's eyes to the photographs of the 1890s graduates in their Edwardian suits and cravats. It almost seemed to Peter that the expression on their faces had turned to incredulity at what they had just observed: a pregnant woman having contractions in the homiletics seminar room.

"The ticking of the clock," said Dorian White Elk, "reminds me of when my wife and I had our firstborn. It was in an old medical mission, and they had a clock with a sound like this one right in the waiting room. I remember our pastor came and prayed with me while she was in delivery. I think we ought to pray for Katherine and for the child who is coming into the world and for Katherine's husband, Richard."

So the five men moved closer to one end of the seminar table and took one another's hands and offered prayers, sometimes speaking out loud, sometimes remaining in silence. When they finished praying, it was clear that class was over for the day. They agreed to go down to the refectory and have some coffee and remember the stories of births in their own families.

Peter stayed behind for a moment to clean up the room. He noticed that Karen had left her sermon manuscript on the seminar table, and as he picked it up, his eye caught some of the lines she had quoted:

> Perhaps the future of institutional Christianity, both in the relations of Christian bodies with each other, and in their relations with other religions and with the world, may be a sacrificial one, abandoning so much the past has cherished in striving to represent the Christ-like spirit.

Karen had a note in the margin indicating that the quotation was from 1990. Peter pulled out a copy of the course syllabus and read once again the 1890s quotation from *The Christian Century*:

We believe that the coming century is to witness greater triumphs
in Christianity than any previous century has ever witnessed, and
that it is to be more truly Christian than any of it predecessors.

The difference in tone and content of the two quotations was
striking. The 1890s quotation started, "We believe," while the
1990s started "Perhaps." The 1890s spoke as though "Christianity" were one unified religious faith, while the 1990s named the
political reality of denominations, talking about the "relations of
Christian bodies with each other." The 1890s foresaw "greater
triumphs in Christianity than any previous century has ever
witnessed" while the 1990s spoke of "abandoning so much the
past has cherished in striving to represent the Christ-like spirit."
The 1890s foresaw a century that was "to be more truly Christian
than any of its predecessors," while the 1990s pondered whether
the relations of Christian bodies "with other religions and with
the world, may be a sacrificial one."

Of course, they were only two quotations, and, of course, one
could probably find authors from the 1890s who sounded like the
1990s and vice versa. Nevertheless, the contrast in tone and content
of the two seemed to capture something of the great homiletical
shift that was sounding in the sermons of Tashika, Katherine,
Marjorie, and Dorian. It was a shift from certitude and triumph to a
faith that was less assured of its earlier absolutism and more open to
other perspectives in the world community.

Peter wondered: "Would such a reevaluation of Christian
belief fuel the church's preaching into the twenty-first century?
Would it awaken faith in the heart of the new child that Katherine
was bringing into the world? Would preachers feel a fire in their
bones to declare a gospel that was open to questioning its own
symbols and traditions? Or were certitude and triumph the
necessary notes of proclamation?"

Chung Won Kim's final sermon for "Preachers in Search of
Their Voices" suggested that the answer to Peter's questions lay
in the fog of the future, as thick as the fog and mist that Chung
Won conjured up as he told Matthew's version of the story of
Jesus' walking on the water.

Throughout the course, Chung Won Kim had often listened
for a long stretch without saying a word, but when he finally
spoke, he revealed that he had taken in the entire discussion. In

the beginning of the course he had observed how everyone brought memories of suffering to the seminar table. Now at the end of the course he gathered together the impact of all their preaching and conversation.

Chung Won began his sermon by telling the class that his tradition considered dreams to be an important source of spiritual insight. He said that if preachers in the Western church wanted to find more effective voices for proclaiming the gospel into the twenty-first century they needed to become more attentive to the world of dreams. "You cannot solve all the great issues of this course by rational argument," Chung Won declared. "You need to balance theological reflection with visions born of the dreams that are stirred by the Spirit."

Then he told the story of a dream that he had after the last class. That evening he had been reading from the Gospel of Matthew as part of another course he was auditing at the seminary, "The Church in the New Testament," but he found the words were not registering in his mind because he was preoccupied with his concern for Kathcrine. So before he went to bed, he called the hospital to find out how Katherine was doing, and he was delighted when Marjorie Hudson came to the phone and said that Katherine had delivered a seven-pound girl, Elizabeth Louise.

"And we're to call her Elizabeth," said Marjorie Hudson. "Her mother says: 'Not Lizzy, like she's some little doll, but Elizabeth, like the great queen of England, strong, regal, and clear headed.'"

That night Chung Won lay awake, praying for Elizabeth Louise and for Katherine. "After I finished praying," Chung Won said, "I recalled my initial reaction to Katherine, when on the first day of class she insisted that we call her Katherine, not Kathy or Kate. I did not have a welcoming spirit in my heart. I thought, and it pains me to acknowledge this now, but I thought, 'Oh no, not another feminist.' And yet here I was four months later lying in bed praying for Katherine and Elizabeth Louise, and I said their whole names to God as I prayed, wanting to make sure that God did not think I was praying for Kate and Liz.

"And as I thought of the change in my attitude toward Katherine and her ideas, I began to realize that I had gone through a similar process again and again in class. Initially, I resisted Marjorie's ideas of focusing on women's experience, I resisted Dorian's plea to get my nose out of the Book and read the land, I resisted that sermon Roger heard that was based on a play rather than Scripture, and I joined the battle with Jason against Tashika's way of dealing with the atonement.

"I did not always express my resistance aloud, but all of these things were going on inside me, the same way they go on in our listeners in our churches, though they never tell us outright. They avert their eyes in the coffee hour, or they take us on about something else in a board meeting.

"So there I am the other night, lying in bed, thinking and praying about all these things until I find myself on a passenger boat in thick fog and mist with a heavy sea. I recognize the small round window in my cabin just below the deck. I'm on the boat that brought my family and me from Korea to America. But I am no longer a little boy. I am the age I am now, and instead of my family, the class is in the boat, and Katherine is just beginning her contractions, and Marjorie is taking control. She asks me to see if I can find the ship's doctor, but when I try to open the door it won't budge because our cabin is on the downward side of a mighty wave, and I am having to lift the door up. I throw my shoulder with my full weight against the door and wake up startled in bed.

"I find I've left my night-light on and my Bible open to Matthew 14:22-33, where Jesus walks upon the water and Peter attempts to walk toward him. Because of what I believe about dreams, I am certain that the Holy Spirit is trying to bring me some revelation, some insight, so I go back and read the passage again.

"I find myself stopping on a verse I must have read a hundred times but that never gripped me so strongly until this very moment: 'But when the disciples saw him walking on the sea, they were terrified, saying, "It is a ghost!" And they cried out in fear.'

"Because I knew the passage was about Jesus' walking on the water I had always skipped over this point in the story. But what an important point it is. In the middle of the storm the disciples did not recognize their Savior. They misidentified him, saying, ' "It is a ghost!" And they cried out in fear.'

"Matthew recorded this story when the church was in stormy seas.[9] Jesus had not returned in the way that the early Christians expected, and the reign of God appeared to be drowning amid the growing persecution of believers and their internal squabbles.

120

"As I thought about that early church, I thought about this class, our common faith and our sharp disagreements. But above all I thought about my resistance to some of you and many of your ideas, and I found myself under the influence of the Holy Spirit, asking: Am I like the disciples in the boat, mistaking as a ghost the one who is my risen Savior?

"Maybe Christ is not coming to us in the way we expect, just as Christ did not come to Matthew's community in the way they expected. Maybe Christ is walking to us across the deep in the ideas and the people who frighten us, who threaten our ideas of how God will be made known.

"Usually, when I preach on this passage, I take the sermon to the conclusion of the story, where Jesus and Peter step into the boat and the wind ceases and the disciples worship their Lord. But through my dream and my study, through our sermons and our debates, I hear the Spirit telling me that we ourselves are only midway into the story. The wind is still blowing, the sea is still tossing, and we fear we see a ghost, something as frightening and unknown as the depths beneath our boat. But that ghostly appearance is perhaps only the veil of fear that we have cast upon our Savior.

"We have a word in the Korean community that describes the tensions we feel in this story of the storm. The word is *han*. *Han* is both scary and yet revealing. It is scary to see how we act out these tensions, how they become part of the conflict between the different generations of Korean immigrants in my church. But *han* is also revealing because it serves, like the storm, to awaken us to Christ, who comes in unexpected ways.[10]

"I am not saying that all storms are good, and I am not saying that I now agree with all that I resisted in 'Preachers in Search of Their Sermons.' But I am making this sacred vow: Before I discount as a ghost any stranger or any idea of God that threatens my own, I shall look out upon the waves and listen by faith to see if I am encountering in unexpected form the one who calls across the deep: 'Take heart, it is I; do not be afraid.' "

Notes

1. Remembered Voices: Recalling the Preachers from Our Past

1. This usage of the word *voice* is common to literary criticism. See Chris Baldick, *The Concise Oxford Dictionary of Literary Terms* (New York: Oxford University Press, 1990), p. 239: "The voice of a literary work is then the specific group of characteristics displayed by the narrator or poetic 'speaker' (or in some uses, the actual author behind them), assessed in terms of tone, style, or personality."

Gardner Taylor describes a variety of great preaching voices he has heard. Nowadays we would want to add to this list examples from women preachers, but Taylor still helps us to understand what the term *voice* means when applied to preachers: "It is a glory of preaching that one text can be given as many different nuances—all of them loyal to the Scriptures—as there are preachers dealing with them. In my years in the City of New York some of the most notable preachers of our generation have been my colleagues, and their memories are still a benediction to me. How different they were and how gloriously did those differences come out in their pulpit work! A sermon of Robert McCracken's invariably reflected the wistful, gently probing makeup of the preacher. In George Buttrick's sermon, one always detected a pursuing logic, a care about simple but eloquent diction and a brooding upon the mystery of godliness and life which were a slice of that preacher's being. Adam Clayton Powell was saucy in temperament and intensely angry about injustice; he also had a lofty concept of Scripture, inherited from his father. Bring those elements together with an almost hypnotic voice, and the resulting sermon is fiery, prophetic, and deeply stirring—particularly to those most closely associated with injustice and hopes long deferred. Paul Scherer was grand and expansive in personality, so his sermons were spacious, sweeping, almost Shakespearean in imaginativeness. The Brooklyn preacher Sandy Ray had a warm, infectious disposition and a genius for finding in Scripture fresh angles of vision often gained from shrewd observations of the human scene. No matter what text he preached, one could see these qualities in his sermon." (Gardner Taylor, "Shaping Sermons by the Shape of Text and Preacher" in Don M. Wardlaw, *Preaching Biblically: Creating Sermons in the Shape of Scripture* [Philadelphia: Westminster Press, 1983], p. 138.)

2. Quoted in Charles H. Lippy, ed., *Religious Periodicals of the U.S.* (Westport, Conn.: Greenwood Press, 1986), p. 110.

3. Sandra M. Schneiders, *Women and the Word* (New York: Paulist Press, 1986), p. 71. Emphasis added.

4. Karl Barth, *The Word of God and the Word of Man*, trans. Douglas Horton (Magnolia, Mass.: Peter Smith, 1958).

5. The words are by Etienne Gilson, *The Spirit of Medieval Philosophy*, pp. 270-72 and are quoted in Reinhold Niebuhr, *The Nature and Destiny of Man*, vol. I (New York: Charles Scribner's Sons, 1964), p. 122.

6. *That Championship Season*, by Jason Miller, won the 1973 Pulitzer Prize in drama. A major motion picture was made a few years ago, and a videotape of this film is available in many video rental shops.

7. The sermon is based on my memory of a sermon I heard preached sometime in the 1970s by Richard L. Manzelmann.

8. Written by Thomas H. Troeger. Though appearing in many hymnals, the poem is originally published in Carol Doran and Thomas H. Troeger, *New Hymns for the Lectionary: To Glorify the Maker's Name* (New York: Oxford University Press, 1986), hymn number 11.

9. Deborah Tannen, *You Just Don't Understand: Women and Men in Conversation* (New York: William Morrow and Company, 1990), p. 95.

10. For a helpful historical summation of the distinctions between the rhetoric of women and men and the long tradition of bias against the use of a so-called "effeminate" style in public speech, see Kathleen Hall Jamieson, *Eloquence in an Electronic Age: The Transformation of Political Speechmaking* (New York: Oxford University Press, 1988), chap. 4, "The 'Effeminate' Style."

11. Fred B. Craddock, *Preaching* (Nashville: Abingdon Press, 1985), pp. 26-27.

12. Cherrie Moraga and Gloria Anzaldua, *This Bridge Called My Back: Writings by Radical Women of Color* (New York: Kitchen Table: Women of Color Press, 1983), p. 72.

2. Neglected Voices: Listening to Outsiders

1. Elisabeth Schüssler Fiorenza, *Bread Not Stone: The Challenge of Feminist Biblical Interpretation* (Boston: Beacon Press, 1984), p. xv. Fiorenza is herself drawing on the work of Marie Augusta Neal, who uses these terms in a different context.

2. I am deeply indebted in this entire section to my colleague, Professor James Poling, who allowed me to read before publication his manuscript *The Abuse of Power: A Theological Problem* (Nashville: Abingdon Press, 1991).

3. Miriam Therese Winter, *WomanWord: A Feminist Lectionary and Psalter, Women of the New Testament* (New York: Crossroad, 1990).

4. For a collection of analytical essays on the way the Bible functions as a symbol in common thought, see Allene Stuart Phy, *The Bible and Popular Culture in America* (Philadelphia: Fortress Press, 1985).

5. Schüssler Fiorenza, *Bread Not Stone*, p. 66.

6. African American spiritual as found in *The United Methodist Hymnal* (Nashville: The United Methodist Publishing House, 1989), hymn number 521.

7. Sallie McFague, *Models of God: Theology for an Ecological, Nuclear Age* (Philadelphia: Fortress Press, 1987), p. 16.

8. Galatians 6:2, J. B. Phillips, *The New Testament in Modern English* (New York: Macmillan, 1962).

9. I am indebted to a former student named Douglas Sullivan for his raising my consciousness about a theology of accessibility through his creative sermons on the topic.

10. I am indebted in this entire section on the inadequacy of a speaking/hearing model for homiletics to Kathy Black of Oakland, California, who sent me the third chapter of the doctoral thesis she is writing on this subject.

11. Jaroslav J. Pelikan and Helmut Lehmann, eds., *Luther's Works*, 55 volumes (St. Louis: Concordia Publishing House, and Philadelphia: Fortress Press, 1955), vol. 29, p. 224.

12. For an analysis of how sign language works and a positive evaluation of deaf culture see David M. Perlmutter, "The Language of the Deaf" in *The New York Review of Books* 28, no. 6, March 28, 1991, pp. 65ff. This extensive article is in part a review of Oliver Sacks, *Seeing Voices: A Journey into the World of the Deaf* (Berkeley: University of California Press, 1989), but the review includes references to many other works on the subject. Perlmutter concludes his article: "What the deaf have to teach us—above all—is that either sign or speech can serve as the vehicle of language. It may take us a long time to assimilate the implications of this simple fact. And it may teach us that there are more ways than we realized of being fully human" (p. 72).

13. I am indebted to my colleague Paul Franklyn for raising this issue in a letter to me.

14. Johann Baptist Metz, *Faith in History & Society: Toward a Practical Fundamental Theology* (New York: The Seabury Press, 1980). This passage and all the other quotations by Metz that follow are from pages 109-10.

15. I am indebted for this analysis to Sung-Kown Oh. I have drawn here from his master's thesis "Paul's Apocalyptic Gospel to the Immigrant Community," at Garrett-Evangelical Theological Seminary, May, 1989, pp. 11-14.

3. New Voices: Gathering Together All We Have Heard

1. Cherrie Moraga, "Refugees of a World on Fire," Foreword to the Second Edition, in Cherrie Moraga and Gloria Anzaldua, eds., *This Bridge Called My Back: Writings by Radical Women of Color* (New York: Kitchen Table: Women of Color Press, 1983), no pagination.

2. See ibid., p. 74.

3. Daniel Iverson, "Spirit of the Living God." See *The United Methodist Hymnal* (Nashville: The United Methodist Publishing House, 1989), hymn number 393.

4. The story is found in Annie Dillard, *The Writing Life* (New York: HarperPerennial, 1989), pp. 8-9.

5. See, for example, Helen Vendler, *New York Times Book Review*, October 14, 1984, p. 41: "The price paid for individuality of voice—the quality, after all, for which we remember poets—is absolute social singularity. Each poet is a species to himself, a mutant in the human herd, speaking an idiolect he shares with no one."

There are challenges to the overindividualization of the writer's voice in some contemporary literary criticism. See, for example, Czeslaw Milosz, *The Witness of Poetry* (Cambridge, Mass.: Harvard University Press, 1983), p. 26: "[Poetry] withdrew from the domain common to all people into the closed circle of subjectivism"; Wendell Berry, *Standing by Words* (San Francisco: North Point Press, 1983), p. 207: "Both the communal and the individual emphases can be carried to extremes, and the extremity of each is loneliness. One can be lonely in the totalitarian crowd, in which no difference is perceived or tolerated; and one can be lonely in the difference or uniqueness of individuality in which community is repudiated."

For specific issues of the impact of gender on voice, see Carol Gilligan, *In a Different Voice: Psychological Theory and Women's Development* (Cambridge, Mass.:

Harvard University Press, 1982), esp. p. 16, where Gilligan discusses the effect of our social propensity to favor male values: "The difficulty women experience in finding or speaking publicly in their own voices emerges repeatedly in the form of qualification and self-doubt, but also in intimations of a divided judgement, a public assessment and private assessment which are fundamentally at odds."

6. For a summation of the complex discussion of the relationship between prophet and cult, see B. D. Napier, "Prophet," in George A. Buttrick, *The Interpreter's Dictionary of the Bible* (Nashville: Abingdon Press, 1962), vol. 3, pp. 900ff.

7. Ibid., vol. 2, p. 704.

8. I am indebted to a sermon preached many years ago by Gardner Taylor for this insight.

9. I am indebted to the Rev. Granville Seward, who related this modern parable to me during a conversation about sermons.

10. See Margaret A. Farley, "Feminist Consciousness and the Interpretation of Scripture," in Letty M. Russell, ed., *Feminist Interpretation of the Bible* (Philadelphia: Westminster Press, 1985).

11. Rachel Blau DuPlessis, "The Critique of Consciousness and Myth in Levertov, Rich, and Rukeyser," *Feminist Studies* 3 (1975): pp. 199-221.

12. Dan Schutte, "Here I Am, Lord." See *The United Methodist Hymnal*, hymn number 593.

13. George Herbert, *The Country Parson* (1652), as found in Richard Lischer, ed., *Theories of Preaching: Selected Readings in the Homiletical Tradition* (Durham, N.C.: The Labyrinth Press, 1989), p. 51.

14. Justo L. González and Catherine G. González, "The Larger Context," in Arthur Van Seters, ed., *Preaching as a Social Act: Theology & Practice* (Nashville: Abingdon Press, 1988), p. 98.

15. For an excellent discussion on the necessity of the preacher's own engagement with the good news, see Henry H. Mitchell, *Celebration and Experience in Preaching* (Nashville: Abingdon Press, 1990), esp. chap. 4, "The Sermon Celebration."

16. Ibid., p. 62.

17. Ibid., p. 66.

18. From a promotional pamphlet of the Society of St. John the Evangelist.

19. Chester P. Michael and Marie C. Norrisey, *Prayer and Temperament: Different Forms of Prayer for Different Personality Types* (Charlottesville, Va.: The Open Door, 1984), p. 16. See also Charles J. Keating, *Who We Are Is How We Pray* (Mystic, Conn.: Twenty-Third Publications, 1988): "We need to develop some of our less favored characteristics if we want to grow more aware and to appreciate the value of others whose personality types are different from our own" (p. 4).

4. The Voice Upon the Deep: Hearing Christ in Unexpected Ways

1. I am indebted here to an actual sermon, which I heard over twenty years ago, by the Rev. George Stiegler, and also to Petru Dumitriu, *To the Unknown God*, trans. James Kirkup (New York: The Seabury Press, 1982), esp. p. 113, where Dumitriu writes: "Ideologies and superstitions, concentration-camp utopias and interplanetary folklore occupy the void left by the withdrawal of the Christian soul and scientific humanism, by the ebbing of Christian intellect and the elitist encystation of men of science in their special languages, waterproof compartments."

2. Thomas H. Troeger, "Silence, Frenzied, Unclean Spirit." See *The United Methodist Hymnal*, hymn number 264.

Notes

3. Vine Deloria, Jr., *Custer Died for Your Sins: An Indian Manifesto* (Norman, Okla.: University of Oklahoma Press, 1988), p. 101.

4. The ideas behind Tashika's sermon were awakened in me through a series of lectures by Delores Williams, which she gave at Colgate Rochester Divinity School/Bexley Hall/Crozer Theological Seminary during the spring term, 1990.

5. I am indebted to my colleague, James Poling, for telling me of case studies where such appeals have actually been made by abusers. See his *The Abuse of Power: A Theological Problem* (Nashville: Abingdon Press, 1991).

6. Francis Schüssler Fiorenza, "Critical Social Theory and Christology: Toward an Understanding of Atonement and Redemption as Emancipatory Solidarity," in *Proceedings of the Thirtieth Annual Convention* of the Catholic Theological Society of America, New Orleans, Louisiana, June 9-12, 1975, vol. 30, pp. 63-110. I am indebted to this entire article for the development of Tashika's sermon on atonement, as well as the phrase and understanding of "emancipatory solidarity."

7. I am indebted for these insights in Karen Steel's sermon to Ann Belford Ulanov, *Picturing God* (Cambridge, Mass.: Cowley Publications, 1986). See especially the essay, "Picturing God," where she writes: "Picturing God must precede any speaking about God, for our pictures accompany all our words and they continue long after we fall silent before God" (p. 164). "To neglect God-images as images means that they are free to gather power to knock us over" (p. 170).

8. John McManners, ed., *The Oxford Illustrated History of Christianity* (New York: Oxford University Press, 1990), from the introduction by the editor, p. 4.

9. See John L. McKenzie, "The Gospel According to Matthew" in Raymond E. Brown, Joseph A. Fitzmyer, Roland E. Murphy, eds., *The Jerome Biblical Commentary* (Englewood Cliffs, N.J.: Prentice-Hall, 1968), p. 89 of the New Testament section: "This chapter [Matthew 14] begins that portion of Mt. that is called the ecclesiastical portion. The disciples in the boat represent, in a not too subtle way, the Church, from which Jesus is never far even when the situation is threatening and he is invisible."

10. I am indebted in creating this part of Chung Won Kim's sermon to Sung-Kown Oh and his Master's thesis, "Paul's Apocalyptic Gospel to the Immigrant Community," Garrett-Evangelical Theological Seminary, May 1989. On pp. 18-19 of his thesis, Sung-Kown Oh quotes from Cyris H. S. Moon, *A Korean Minjung Theology: An Old Testament Perspective* (Maryknoll, N.Y.: Orbis Books, 1985), p. 2: "Through the experience of the han one's spiritual eyes are opened and one is enabled to see the deep truths about life. In han, we come to see the infinite value of personhood and are able to assert our precious right as human beings. In han we see clearly what is good and evil and learn to hate evil and love good. In han we encounter God who comes down to the han-ridden people and justifies their plight. With han as our point of departure we begin to dream of a new, alternative future and to dedicate ourselves to the cause of making that future a reality."

Index

General

Acid rain, resemblance to preaching, 28

Atonement, 107, 109

Barth, Karl, 23
Benson, Richard Meux, 89
Bread Not Stone: The Challenge of Feminist Biblical Interpretation (Schüssler Fiorenza), 41, 43, 45, 79

Christian Century, 13-14, 117
Christmas, 16, 22
Craddock, Fred, 35
Cross, 104-11

Deafness, 56-58
Dillard, Annie, 124

Faith in History and Society (Metz), 64, 65
Feminism, 16-17, 41-43

Gilson, Etienne, 123
Good Samaritan, 76-79

Han, 121
Herbert, George, 81
"Here I Am, Lord," 81
Holiness tradition, 59-61
Holy Spirit, 24-25, 60, 62, 69, 74, 98-100

"I Want Jesus to Walk with Me," 45

"Jesus Loves Me," 55

McFague, Sallie, 50
Memories, subversive, 65-66
Metz, Johann Baptist, 64-65
Mitchell, Henry, 86
Models of God: Theology for an Ecological, Nuclear Age (McFague), 50
Moraga, Cherrie, 36, 68

Niebuhr, Reinhold, 30

Oxford Illustrated History of Christianity, The, 115

Pentecost, 24, 34
Power, nature of, 50
Prayer and Temperament: Different Forms of Prayer for Different Personality Types (Michael and Norrisey), 90
Preaching (Craddock), 35

Rabbi Uri of Strelisk, 70
Rhetoric, male bias, 123

Schneiders, Sandra, 17-18
Schüssler Fiorenza, Elisabeth, 41, 43, 45, 79

Second Coming, 32, 33
"Silence, Frenzied, Unclean Spirit," 96
Slavery, 45
"Spirit of the Living God, Fall Afresh on Me," 69, 71

Tannen, Deborah, 34
Taylor, Gardner, 122
That Championship Season, 31, 65
Theology of relinquishment, 44
Theology of self-affirmation, 42-44
This Bridge Called My Back: Writings by Radical Women of Color (Moraga and Anzaldua), 36, 68

United Methodist Hymnal, The, 16

Voice of God, 73, 81
Voice of preacher, 13

War, 22, 46, 63-64, 105, 112
"When I Survey the Wondrous Cross," 111
"Wind Who Makes All Winds That Blow," 34
Woman, battered, 40-42
Women and the Word (Schneiders), 17-18
Women in conversation, 34

Yeats, William Butler, 32, 33
You Just Don't Understand: Men and Women in Conversation (Tannen), 34

Scripture

Psalms

11.....113
78.....82

Isaiah

11.....23
55.....48, 49

Luke

10:25-37.....76
17:2.....107

Acts

2.....98
20.....24

Romans

10:17.....56
12:2.....87-88

2 Corinthians

5:17.....41

Galatians

6:2.....53

1 Peter

2:9.....60